Beautiful Merchandise:
Prostitution in China
1860–1936

About the Author

Sue Gronewold is completing her doctoral work in Chinese history at Columbia University. She is the lecturer on Asia at the American Museum of Natural History, New York City, and a member of the Institute for Research in History.

Beautiful Merchandise: Prostitution in China 1860–1936

Sue Gronewold

Beautiful Merchandise: Prostitution in China 1860–1936 was originally published in 1982 by The Haworth Press, Inc. It has also been published as *Women & History*, Number 1, Spring 1982.

Harrington Park Press
New York • Binghamton

ISBN 0-918393-15-9

Published by

Harrington Park Press, Inc.
28 East 22 Street
New York, New York 10010

Harrington Park Press, Inc., is a subsidiary of The Haworth Press, Inc., 28 East 22 Street, New York, New York 10010.

Beautiful Merchandise: Prostitution in China 1860–1936 was originally published in 1982 by The Haworth Press, Inc., under the same title. It has also been published as *Women & History,* Number 1, Spring 1982.

Library of Congress Cataloging in Publication Data

Gronewold, Sue.
    Beautiful merchandise.

    Bibliography: p.
    Includes index.
    1. Prostitution—China—History. I. Title.
HQ250.A5G76   1985   306.7'42'0951   85-7672
ISBN 0-918393-15-9 (pbk.)

CONTENTS

FOREWORD

The appearance of this first issue of *Women & History* is a sign of the coming of age of women's history. After more than a decade of intensive research, increasing scholarly output, and the proliferation of women's history courses on the undergraduate, graduate, and secondary school levels, the time has surely come for a journal devoted solely to the history of women.

Women & History is different from traditional historical journals in several respects. Instead of short articles, it will present monographs and collections of longer-than-usual essays focused on a central theme—the kind of in-depth studies essential to the development of any scholarly discipline. Moreover, the research published in *Women & History* will reflect the diversity of women's historical experiences and the broad range of scholarship in women's history. We welcome contributions by historians of all periods, geographical areas, cultures, and methodological approaches—social, cultural, political, and intellectual history, the history of religion, labor history, family history, and especially comparative and cross-cultural studies. Most importantly, perhaps, we welcome the opportunity to publish the work of young as well as established scholars, of historians outside as well as inside academia.

For over a decade historians of women have been helping one another discover how to study women and sharing their insights and information. As a result, we are beginning to build a real history of women—to see the flow of events over time, to discern continuities and discontinuities, and to discover similarities and differences among women's experiences in different cultures and ages. By publishing *Women & History*, the Institute for Research in History and The Haworth Press hope, above all, to further this endeavor: our goal is to help illuminate women's past in all its richness, variety, and complexity.

We are very fortunate to begin *Women & History* with Sue Gronewold's *Beautiful Merchandise: Prostitution in China 1860–1936*. Not only does it reflect the goals of the series, but it is a fine example of the fresh, lively, and meticulous research being conducted by young scholars in many areas of women's history. Moreover, Gronewold addresses questions of interest to increasing numbers of historians of the West as well as the East—questions concerning the interrelationships between sexual ideology, class, family, and politics.

Gronewold's study is set in the fascinating and exotic (for westerners) world of pre-revolutionary China. Through the skillful use of an extraordinarily wide variety of sources—novels and short stories, biographies, government documents, newspapers, magazines, law codes, statistical studies, missionary and social scientists' reports, and the observations of foreign visitors—she presents a vivid picture of the daily lives and life cycles of prostitutes and demonstrates how prostitution changed in China from late Imperial times through the Republican period. Most importantly, she demonstrates that prostitution was just one aspect—albeit an extreme one—of an economy in women that pervaded Chinese society; an economy in which women and female children were regularly sold, traded, pawned, and adopted as servants, slaves, brides, foster daughters, concubines—and prostitutes.

Gronewold clearly shows how this economy was rooted in and maintained by Chinese notions of propriety and sexual conduct, class and family structure, political processes, and economic organization. This economy was highly sensitive to the major economic and political stresses of the period and prostitution, in particular, underwent some significant changes during this turbulent epoch in Chinese history. But despite the fall of the Empire, attempts at political and social reform, increasing urbanization, and cultural incursions from the West, the bases of the economy in women, though somewhat altered, remained fundamentally unchanged. At the moment of Mao's revolution, women of all classes remained "merchandise" in a sexual economy enmeshed in the very fabric of Chinese culture and society.

Clearly there is much here to interest Chinese and western scholars, political and economic historians, historians of the family, and, of course, all those historians of women seeking a broader understanding of some of the most vital questions confronting women's history today.

Eleanor S. Riemer
April, 1982

Beautiful Merchandise: Prostitution in China 1860–1936

CHAPTER ONE: POWDER FACES AND WILD CHICKENS:
Chinese Prostitution 1860–1911

Introduction

In the nineteenth century, westerners were often struck by the difference between the "social evil" in China and the West. They found in China no lewd streetwalkers or sordid side streets filled with brothels, no blatant attempts to advertise or seduce customers on roadways or brothel quarters, no evidence of rough pimps who blackmailed customers and pummeled recalcitrant "johns" and their women. Instead, they discovered magical pleasure boats and tea-houses filled with sophisticated ladies whose primary function was entertainment.

The most immediate problem for the historian attempting to understand this most unusual institution and trace its roots in Chinese society is to locate reliable historical sources. One potentially rich body of material is the writings of the literate elite, especially their memoirs and reminiscences. Nostalgia for the splendors of past eras is a familiar theme in Chinese literature. At the end of the Ming dynasty (1368–1644) and during the Ch'ing dynasty (1644–1912), reminiscences written by the literati recaptured their carefree youth squandered in drinking and making merry in the brothel districts of Peking, Nanking, Canton, or Soochow. From their lamentations about the disappearance of "wine and flower days" we can glean a great deal of information about prostitution, although the more sordid or mundane details were of course omitted.[1] There also was a thriving tradition of erotic and pornographic literature in China in this period. The underground novels, paintings, and other erotica that were privately enjoyed by the literate elite were unusually bawdy and explicit, and offer us another rich source of information.[2]

The end of the Ch'ing and the turbulent early Republican period that began in 1912 evoked wildly varied responses from intellectuals. Some evinced the same nostalgia as earlier writers for times

gone by, but many more were modernists who criticized the evils
and backwardness of the decaying empire. Their novels did not
recall youthful indulgences and prostitution for their delights but as
symbols of the nation's poverty, corruption, and decadence.[3] These
"blame" novels stressed the more sordid aspects in society that
reinforced prostitution, and therefore provide a rich source of material for the social historian. Of course one must be cautious about
accepting the moral exhortations in this literature as accurate reflec-
tions of contemporary views. But the background details inserted by
authors to authenticate place and character are very valuable. Descriptions of clothing and personal appearance, references to prices,
and the myriad of small details these authors use to situate their
works are important pieces of historical evidence to which can be
applied the tests used for other kinds of documentation.

Unfortunately, the Ch'ing dynasty was characterized by increasing prudishness and the censorship of erotic subjects. Thus, the
historian must often turn to western sources for reliable details
about life in the prostitution compounds in the nineteenth century.
Since to travel to China has always been to write about it, the
historian can refer to the large number of observations on Chinese
society by western missionaries, scholars, diplomats, and businessmen. Care must be taken, however, to note their cultural blinders
and ulterior motives concerning capitalism and Christianity.

By a judicious use of these and other sources, one can begin to
piece together the prostitute's story. In many ways it was not a
pretty one. Behind the elegant carved facades of the pleasure boats
and within the more sordid "white houses" were women whose lives
were hardly all wine and flowers. Some might enjoy a few years as
celebrated courtesans and some were rescued by marriage, but most
were not so fortunate. This study will attempt to tell their whole
story from childhood to old age, from elite courtesan to her lower-
class sister as well. It will focus less on the delights and degradations
of "the life" than on the sexual economy that it reflected and the
female life cycle that framed it.

The study of prostitution in China offers us valuable new perspectives on some of the most controversial issues for Chinese historians
today. The increasing immiseration of the countryside, the nature of
rural and urban linkages, rural and urban stratification, and the
character of local elites are all reflected in the prostitute's mirror.
Furthermore, studying the déclassés in any society can tell us a great

deal about the respectable, about their mentality, morality, and even their attitudes about social control and mobility.

More particularly, the study of prostitution in China can give us insights into the status of women and the decisions families made concerning their females. Throughout history most prostitutes have been female and most clients male, linked in sexual relations by an economic nexus. As a consequence, this topic is not only linked with the role and status of women, but is also connected with lifestyles and family economies that involved men as well. Most importantly, prostitution was not merely the destiny of a few outcasts. Prostitution was a reality for thousands of Chinese women in the nineteenth and twentieth centuries and a threat for many others, particularly those who were poor. Men at all levels of society were involved in the sale and purchase of women. The study of prostitution, therefore, can illuminate the lives of Chinese women who never passed the portal of a brothel and of the men who helped shape their lives.

In sum, then, the task for a social historian is a compelling one. Prostitution impinged upon all segments of society in a wide variety of ways, recruiting its victims and procurers most often from the poor, while the middlemen and clients came from all segments of the population. Only by examining what the institution once represented in Chinese history, can we understand what it had become by the early decades of the twentieth century. Then one can begin to comprehend both the hidden fury of ordinary women traditionally treated like property and the smouldering resentment of submissive "songstresses" confined to brothels.

The central argument of this study is that the purchase of women for prostitution was not qualitatively different from the general trade in women that existed in China. Among all classes, females were viewed as more disposable than males. Were they not, after all, destined to leave the family hearth when their childhood years were over, belonging no longer to their natal family but to a stranger's family instead? In times of economic strife, hard-pressed parents sought ways to hasten the departure of females, and a virtual marketing of women developed. Throughout Chinese history, females were limited, restricted, and reduced to property. They were purchased as wives and concubines, servants and slaves—and as prostitutes. Merchandise, then, is more than a mere metaphor of women's fate in China. A study of "beautiful merchandise"—one

Chinese euphemism for prostitution[4]—can illustrate the manners, morals, and economy of the Chinese people.

History of Prostitution

Prostitution existed in China from the dawn of recorded history. Historical and mythological tales from the Shang dynasty (1523–1028 B.C.) suggest that royalty employed singing troupes (*nü-yueh*), entertainers who probably also served as prostitutes.[5] According to tradition, the first brothels open to a wider public were introduced by a minister of the state of Ch'i in the seventh century B.C. Brothel keepers were licensed and taxes gathered. In the first century B.C., Emperor Wu of the Han dynasty (202 B.C.–220 A.D.) permitted brothels to be established near army camps and filled them with female felons, relatives of criminals, and prisoners of war. At the same time, the number of public brothels increased and private singing troupes declined, while courtesans increasingly functioned both as entertainers and sexual instructors. Since they often were among the few women who were literate, courtesans could draw on a growing body of sex manuals describing Taoist mystical techniques.[6]

Independent streetwalkers do not seem to have been common at any time in Chinese history. Women and clients alike appear to have preferred the structure and security of routinized brothel life. This preference was soon supported by a web of custom, tradition, and law which continued until the twentieth century. By the T'ang dynasty (618–906 A.D.), brothels seem to have been licensed by the state and organized into three classes, or levels, each with its own recruitment, customs, and clientele.[7]

From the first descriptions of public prostitution, it appears that very early in Chinese history certain basic principles were established and special linkages were made: (1) public prostitution was not only accepted by the state but was used directly or indirectly as a source of revenue; (2) public prostitution was not closely connected with religion, as in ancient Greece or Rome, but with the arts and entertainment, such as dancing, singing, and design; (3) the demand for prostitution in any period was tied closely to the fate of the merchant middle strata who desired lavish, conspicuous entertainment; (4) the supply of prostitution at any time was intimately connected with the amount of social and economic dislocation; and (5) the public ideology was always Janus-faced. Confucian (and later Buddhist) moral condemnation coexisted with an attitude of acceptance.

Courtesans, the elite of the profession, were not viewed as eternally fallen, sinful women. Instead, as long as they obeyed the rules of propriety they were welcomed by the elite as a complement to the institution of marriage and were considered suitable candidates for secondary wives. Once married, they could lead respectable lives. Lower-class prostitutes, on the other hand, had a disreputable image—a function of their class more than of their occupation.

Five Streets and Seven Lanes

The Chinese brothels, in large part an urban phenomenon, were known as *ch'ing lou* ("blue houses" or "green bowers"), after the custom of painting the shutters to advertise the establishment's services. These houses were divided into three or four classes, depending on the municipality. Before the eighteenth century, brothels were generally restricted to special quarters of the cities. During the eighteenth and nineteenth centuries restrictions were relaxed. European visitors were shocked to find brothels "everywhere,"[8] but most cities retained three (or four) classes of brothels. The houses were licensed by municipal authorities, and prostitutes were issued permits restricting them to establishments within a particular class.[9]

The highest level brothels, called *ke kuan* (sing-song houses) or *ch'a fang* (teahouses), housed courtesans, the elite of the profession. These upper-class establishments were luxurious and expensive; they usually contained many rooms on a single floor, with separate chambers arranged around a common room which was luxuriously decorated. In Canton, these establishments often had two stories, with the individual rooms around a salon on the upper floor. A special password was often required to enter; no exterior sign indicated that this was indeed a brothel. The courtesans, elegantly dressed and coiffured, displayed small bound feet and were skilled in entertainment arts. Sexual relations were permitted only after a long and quite costly period of courtship. The clientele of these houses were usually high officials, wealthy merchants, wealthy scholars, and artists.

The second category were outright brothels, or wine houses (*chiu kuan*), restaurants, or taverns that had singing girls connected to them. The prostitutes in these houses, too, were skilled in both entertainment and sexual techniques, but the establishments were not nearly as lavish or exclusive as those of the first class. Here, the entrance way was often ornately decorated and inscribed with the house's poetic name, such as "Temple of Supreme Happiness" or "Garden of Perfumed Flowers." A sign designated the class of the house, and slips of paper hung near the door bore the "flower name" of each inhabitant. Customers were further enticed to enter by the sounds of music—flute or fiddle—wafting out, or the sight of women peering out of upper windows or leaning against the balcony, dressed in gaudy clothes with brightly painted faces. Sex was available more readily in second-class houses, and clients could stay the night on the first few visits. The clientele of these houses were for the most part lower officials and middle-level scholars and merchants.

The third category consisted of inexpensive brothels whose women had scant training, if any, in entertainment skills. These houses contained a few barely furnished rooms and provided cheap, quick, and convenient sex for poor men, soldiers, and young scholars going "slumming." Much of the clientele consisted of poor urban workers or travellers from surrounding villages. Many of those men had not married because they could not pay for a bride and because of the scarcity of women for partners. According to contemporary sources, the customers were often so numerous that they formed lines outside to wait—and even watch.[10]

Many establishments, especially those in this third class, had traditionally been government run and staffed, but that practice seems to have declined during the Ch'ing dynasty, except for barracks prostitution. Brothels were privately owned and staffed, and a large number of brothels had only a few prostitutes; one reliable source cites the case of a man having a brothel with only two "sisters." Western travellers frequently remarked on size as a striking difference betwen the brothels in China and the West.[11]

Flower boats, *hua fang,* were floating brothels anchored along the waterways of South and Central China. They were grouped together by class and sometimes also according to the province or city of origin of their personnel.[12] Generally, the women did not reside on these boats but came only in the afternoon or evening for the day's entertainment. The boats, sixty to eighty feet long and approximately fifteen feet wide, usually contained two large com-

FIGURE 1. A Cantonese flower boat of the 1870s. (Reprinted by permission of the Peabody Museum of Salem)

7

partments in the center surrounded by walkways along the side. One compartment was open for feasts and entertainment, and an inner compartment was fitted with beds and couches for "fooling with the girls"[13] and opium smoking. Provisions could be made for staying the night either in a small loft provided for that purpose or in smaller boats anchored nearby. Boats were anchored next to one another with a kitchen boat often placed strategically in the middle. The most luxurious were elaborately furnished with rosewood and ebony tables and chairs, tapestries and velvet curtains or even European chandeliers. Less opulent boats were smaller but had comfortable furnishings with a smaller number of rooms and multi-colored lanterns that twinkled in the night, producing a magical effect.[14] A Chinese writer eulogized the flourishing of lantern boats along Nanking's Ch'in Huai River as "unmatched throughout the universe," and even staid American missionaries were often awestruck by their soft, luminous glow.[15]

Lastly, there were some prostitutes without brothels, and open solicitation, while rare, did occur. Yet even these women, mostly beggar women in the poor quarters and women attached to post stations, seem to have had some loose organization under a madam or beggar "king."[16]

Organization and Personnel

Some form of entertainment began the afternoon or evening's routine in nearly all first- or second-class brothels, those on land as well as on water. Clients came alone, with one or two friends, or in groups of from ten to twenty. Larger parties were encouraged by upper-class houses, since they gave courtesans and houses more "face" and, of course, profits. Women in the most luxurious houses, like western call girls, were not subjected to a selection process but instead could decide whom to accept or refuse. If the guests had visited previously, they expected to be served by the same women as before, or they might bring women with them from other establishments to join in a feast. If it were a first visit, unassigned women were introduced and the clients made their selections. Each guest was assigned one woman to serve him for the visit; if it were a lower-class brothel, sex was the aim and women led the clients to their individual cabinets, although sometimes there may have been perfunctory feasting, singing, or instrument playing. The routine was very different in the wine houses, teahouses, or upper-level flower boats. There, an elaborate feast lasting several hours and interspersed with singing and instrument playing by the female attendants consumed the major portion of the visit. The sing-song girl's main function was to sit next to and serve her client, offering him food, wine, and pipes while taking very little for herself. Musicians, attached either to the dinner party or the individual women, serenaded the guests before, during, and after the feasting. Once the wine drinking and eating were over, social games such as the popular finger game or chess were played, special folk songs or opera selections were sung, opium was smoked, or if it were a floating brothel, a tour was made around the other flower boats.[17]

One variation of this sort of evening's festivities was the rental of women and attendants from "flower houses" or "flower boats" to prepare a "flower banquet" in the home of a wealthy official or merchant. For these evenings, male singers and actors might be hired, and the women of the household, ordinarily absent from the men's social gatherings, might be allowed to join in.

Brothel personnel had clearly differentiated functions and titles which mirrored kinship relations, in fancy, if not usually in fact. Brothels and teahouses were usually owned by a man, called *lao papa* (father) by the inmates or, more vulgarly, *piao t'ou* (boss of a whorehouse), by outsiders. The manager was usually a woman who herself had been a prostitute for many years. The madam was known to the brothel women as *lao mama* (mother), but was given the vulgar name by outsiders of *lao pao* (old bird), a derogatory term since the *pao* bird was regarded as a particularly licentious creature. Occasionally the fictive kinship relationship was modified, and madams were called *chia mu* (adopted mother) and prostitutes, "foster daughters." Madams of other houses were referred to as "aunts," and they in turn referred to the prostitutes of other brothels as their "nieces." Prostitutes referred to their own colleagues as "sisters" and those of other establishments as "cousins," while the guests themselves were called "husbands" and "brothers-in-law."[18]

Although called "daughter" by madams, the prostitutes were given a bewildering variety of labels by the public. These terms ranged from the gentler, more euphemistic titles of "flower girl" (*hua niang*) and "powder face" (*fen t'ou*) to the more vulgar term *piao* (whore). Women of lower houses were also referred to as "willows on the road and flowers on the wall," to suggest their easy availability, while those not attached to any establishment were derogatorily called "wild chickens" (*yeh chi*).[19] It seems that the more euphemistic terms were reserved for upper-class courtesans, while lower-class prostitutes were labeled with the most derisive of titles.

Each house had its share of servants, and in the better establishments these maids and servants were differentiated according to several specializations. Each prostitute had her own private maid; the house also had cooks, water and pipe carriers, preparers of the alum water used for bathing, and bouncers for quieting disputes or ejecting recalcitrant guests. Whole retinues of tutors and musicians were employed by upper-class houses, and often these instructors, like the madams, were older prostitutes no longer willing or able to service clients.[20] Only the servants and other assorted staff members were exempt from the kinship terminology. They referred to the prostitutes more distantly by the equivalent of "ma'am." Thus, the brothel attempted to reproduce the family that shaped the rest of society and so render itself both familiar and legitimate.

Prices and Population

The expenses for a visit to the brothels of "willow lane" varied according to the location and class of house. Chinese authors and foreign travellers usually were far less interested than the twentieth-century "participant observers" and social surveyors in recording such mundane details as cost, but there are occasional references in the literature. One night might be extremely expensive. The Ch'ing "courtesan" novel *Nine Tailed Tortoise* noted that the "courtship" for one night with a renowned courtesan might cost as much as an accumulated $3-4,000[21] and require many months of presents and favors. (All monetary amounts have been converted to their value in U.S. dollars at that time.)[22] A Dutch physician, Dr. Gustaaf Schlegel, in detailed observations of Cantonese flower boats and the brothels of Amoy province made in 1869, noted that the entire cost of a "flower banquet," including lights, drinks, attendants, and dinner, might be as much as four to six pounds ($40-60) per person. Other foreign observers noted the widespread availability of women for just a few coins, but these accounts probably refer to the lowest class brothels or those established expecially for the foreign community.[23] Two Chinese "blame" novels, whose narrators are innocents gradually discovering the evils of their society, provide additional information. In *Vignettes of the Late Ch'ing,* a rustic spends one night in a lower-class brothel "for only a few *yuan,*" perhaps $.75. Prostitutes in *The Travels of Lao Ts'an* ask for only a few *taels* for themselves, perhaps $1.00 to $1.50.[24] In *The Daughter of Han,* the moving autobiography of a woman from North China at the turn of the century, Old Lady Ning tells of a prostitute in a small town who would grant sexual favors to any man for as little as three coppers[25] (approximately three-tenths of a cent). Generally, prostitutes saw very little of this money. If they had been purchased as slaves, all of it was taken by the manager of their house. But even if they were legally free, they might have had to hand over their earnings to managers, servants, attendants, or their families. Ch'ing writers were generally mute about the actual extent of prostitution, so we know almost as little about numbers for the nineteenth century as for earlier periods.[26] "A distant town" mentioned in the seventeenth century realistic novel *Golden Lotus* boasted 72 brothels,[27] and seventeen brothels were listed by Howard Levy as belonging to the prostitution compound in Nanking in the sixteenth century.[28] On the other hand, Dr. Schlegel quoted an 1861 report claiming Amoy contained 3,658 brothels with 25,000 prostitutes in a population of 300,000, but this number appeared excessive to him.[29]

Recruitment

Fortunately, the available sources tell us a great deal about those people who ran, owned, and supplied brothels, and thus about brothel life and recruitment practices. It appears that the social class of a brothel owner tended to parallel the class of his brothel or inn. Nevertheless, involvement with brothel ownership was considered disreputable. Owners of the upper-class restaurants that housed courtesans generally were merchants, often parvenus desiring profitable ways to invest their newly accumulated wealth. Often these men had connections with lower-level officials or gangsters. In *Vignettes,* when an official was demoted five ranks, it was assumed that it would make him a brothel keeper, the lowest position possible for a man.[30] All that was required, it seems, to operate a brothel was a little extra capital and the desire to make a quick turn on a rather shady investment.

Managers of brothels tended to have even less status. In fact, most were women of disreputable background. Generally, madams of brothels proper were ex-prostitutes; managers of small teahouses were sometimes local unattached women involved in other shady dealings. These brothels and teahouses often camouflaged gambling operations, secret rendezvous for the unmarried and the adulterous, or a trade in women. Frequently, these madams were local procuresses who had access to the segregated women's quarters in private homes by acting or posing as hairdressers, nuns, sellers of trinkets, matchmakers, or footbinders.[31]

Brothels were usually supplied with women by men whose major income came from trading in humans. But they are a much more elusive group than the procuresses, who were known in their localities. Many seem to have been from the world of free-floating unemployed men, those without families or who had left their families in hard times and drifted about the cities and countryside doing brief menial contract work. Many of these men moved in and out of procuring. On the other hand, many legitimately employed men, such as hotel managers, and even highly placed officials, such as military officials and magistrates, were extensively involved in the sale of women. For them procuring represented another tolerated form of "squeeze."[32]

Prostitutes were obtained for brothels by four major methods: purchase and pawning from relatives, often through a middleman who concealed the true purpose of the sale or pawn; kidnapping; "free choice;" or government decree, usually as a criminal punishment. Purchase was by far the most frequent method. Lower-class brothels tended to be filled with rejects from upper-level houses, those women who were too old or poor, too unattractive or unskilled to bring in sufficient money, and so had been sold down the brothel ladder for a small sum. Lower-class brothels also contained women who had been remanded to them by government action as punishment for criminal behavior or because they were the relatives of criminals or prisoners of war. There are also some references to unattached women freely entering lower-class houses, in part due to the lack of other employment options for unskilled women and also to the relative secrecy that this life afforded them. Escaped concubines who had been ill-treated were one sort of volunteer; beggars and destitute women were another. These women all shared a lack of attractiveness as entertainers, which reduced them to simply serving clients' sexual needs.[33]

Middle- and upper-class brothels, restaurants, and teahouses secured their women in a variety of ways. Networks of kidnappers, often roving bandits or unemployed or underemployed city men looking for an easy source of income, abducted women and girls "of good families." Sometimes the victims were directly put to work for the kidnappers. More often they were offered for ransom and, if none was forthcoming, were sold for a high price to brothels or procurers.[34] Women were also obtained by raids on neighboring states (Indochina was a popular source of reputedly beautiful prostitutes) and minority groups within China, such as the Hakkas.[35]

The purchase of women for prostitution was a complex affair, which was made even more complicated by the practice of relatives pawning women, including wives, with the professed hope of eventually redeeming them. These twin phenomena were not restricted to rural or urban, Han or ethnic, northern or southern Chinese; women appear to have been purchased and pawned everywhere in China. They were sent to private homes as adopted daughters, future brides, concubines, servants, and slaves. Since prostitution was a dishonorable career, most prostitute purchasers carefully camouflaged the intended outcome of the sale or pawn and instead offered bogus domestic positions, marriage partners, or familial placements. The parents and relatives who sold these women were doubly cheated: not only were their wives and daughters resold into a dishonorable profession, but they were not even able to benefit from the often considerable profits of the sale.

Life Cycle

The life cycle as well as the price of a typical prostitute varied according to the class of house to which she belonged. Those in the upper- and middle-class houses tended to follow the same trajectory. Usually they were bought at a young age (generally under six years old) from poor families or from procurers or middlemen who had purchased them. In the most elite houses, attractive girls of seven or eight would undergo the painful process of footbinding. Since footbinding commenced at this age, older girls, unless their feet were bound, were not purchased for these houses. The girls were then put to work doing menial tasks in the house, either acting as servants for the older women or serving tea and pipes to customers.

Towards eleven years of age, professional education and training

FIGURE 2. Courtesan, c. 1875. Note her small bound feet. (Reprinted from *The Face of China As Seen by Photographers and Travelers 1860–1912*, copyright © 1978 Aperture, Inc., p. 42.)

began. The girls were given singing lessons and instruction on the lute, the *p'i-p'a,* and if they proved quick and unusually talented were taught reading and writing, calligraphy, painting, chess playing, and verse composition. By age thirteen they would be more explicitly prepared as sexual entertainers. They were taught how to retain their composure while drinking and dining and how to handle customers in such a way as to get the most profit. They were trained to spot a provincial who could be easily taken, to enjoy scholars without falling in love, and to locate and catch the most attractive of clients: wealthy, older, well-placed men searching for concubines. With the aid of the age-old traditions found in sex manuals, erotic paintings, and pamphlets, they were given detailed instruction in the "Art of the Bedchamber," including the use of aphrodisiacs and other sexual devices.[36]

Between the ages of thirteen and fifteen they would be sold for the first time to a customer. Since Chinese men placed an extraordinarily high value on virginity, this first sale was much sought after. It was, in fact, one of two occasions on which managers and owners could immediately recoup their investment in a woman (sale as a concubine was the other). The defloration was generally called "combing the hair" but, according to Dr. Schlegel, had special names assigned to it, depending on the age at which it was done. If it occurred at age thirteen, it was termed "trying out the flower," if at age fourteen it was "blossoming of the flower," and by age fifteen, it was known under the more general term of "picking the flower."[37] The defloration was an occasion for grand festivities which could last from two weeks to two months. Women from other brothels often joined in the celebrations. For this "joyous" occasion, a customer was expected to pay from 90 to 1500 florins ($30-450). Yet the importance of the first sale was not merely financial. Often done with all the trappings of a wedding feast, the occasion allowed the couple to be referred to as "bride" and "groom," thus once again legitimizing prostitution by mimicking familial relationships.

After this *rite de passage,* the prostitute was considered a bona fide member of the house and was given her own chambers, servants, and customers. However, managers frequently deceived customers by offering a regular prostitute as a virgin, perhaps dozens of times. In these instances, chicken blood was used to supply the desired evidence of virginity. Each locale had its own terminology for these "two-time women," as well as for the deflowered prostitute considered ready for business.[38]

Chances for upward mobility for prostitutes in upper-class houses were better than for those in lower-class houses. The one great hope of all prostitutes—to become a rich man's secondary wife—was far more possible for courtesans since some men seemed to regard upper-class brothels as concubine markets.[39]

If they were especially skillful, older women of the better houses might be kept on as tutors or procuresses. If they were particularly adept and intelligent, they might be able to move into the position of manager-madam. According to Dr. Schlegel, this was a more realistic expectation for most prostitutes than marriage.[40] If women were far-sighted and successful, they might purchase their freedom from the owner, move out of the brothel, and set up independent housekeeping. As free women they might marry or just live out the rest of their lives with natural or adopted daughters to care for them.

But the fate of most prostitutes, once their attractiveness had faded, was to descend the brothel ladder by being sold to progressively lower houses. Those in the lower-class brothels were eventually thrown out on the streets once they ceased attracting customers. This route, in fact, was the destiny of the large majority of prostitutes, even though most probably held onto the hope of moving out or upward. Old age signalled the end of a prostitute's career in the brothel. The unfortunate majority ended their days either by continuing to hawk their aged and diseased bodies on the street for only a few coppers, by begging, or by turning to some street profession such as seamstress, repairing soldiers' and coolies' clothing for a pittance.[41]

The ultimate fate of most prostitutes was to be poor, aged, and alone. But what can we say about the general experience of prostitutes in their most active years? We can deduce from our nineteenth century eyewitness accounts that there was, not surprisingly, a variation in treatment and condition paralleling the class of brothels. Of course, there were always anomalies—upper-class houses run by harsh madams and lower-class establishments whose operators were models of kindness. In general, however, it behooved managers of courtesans to treat their merchandise well. But lower-class proprietors were aware that their personnel had little attraction for customers. Thus, to realize a profit they overworked them and provided only bare subsistence. Since brothel owners and operators were responsible for prostitutes' food and clothing, this treatment was reflected in their appearance. Observers marvelled at the luxurious clothing, jewelry, elaborate coiffures, and sedan chair rides of the elite courtesans, while women of the lower-class brothels were usually unattractive and wore either garish clothing and cosmetics or poor, thin suits.[42]

Courtesans not only received whom they wished, they also participated to some degree in the festivals and family celebrations of elite society. They were employed in private homes at birthday celebrations and at festivities marking the birth of a son, an official appointment or honor. They were regular participants at weddings; they escorted the bride from her home to her parents-in-law's and instructed the marital couple in sexual techniques.[43] Important roles in parades were reserved for courtesans in the annual cycle of festivals. Lower-class prostitutes, on the other hand, were either imprisoned in brothels or were put on view only as an advertisement.

Appearances, however, were deceptive. Often they camouflaged ill-treatment. Managers frequently physically abused a woman who was unable to attract customers, tried to run away or hide money, or whose customer absconded without payment. Fights among clients and abuse by customers, although more common in lower-class brothels, frequently occurred in upper-class houses as well. At all levels control was also maintained by the practice of encouraging indebtedness to the owners. Proprietors appealed to prostitutes' low self-esteem and *ennui* by offering all manner of trinkets, from hair ornaments and silks to alcohol and opium. As a result, indebtedness often became overwhelming and the possibility of freedom remote.[44]

Occupational Hazards

Physical abuse was only one of the dangers inherent in the profession; there were other occupational hazards for a prostitute, including venereal disease, pregnancy, abortion and addiction to alcohol and opium. Gonorrhea seems to have existed in China from earliest recorded history, but habits of extreme cleanliness by both prostitutes and customers managed to check it so that it was not perceived as a danger. Many of the illnesses and deaths attributed in literature to an overindulgence in sex or "overheating of the system," such as in the seventeenth century novel *Golden Lotus* and the great eighteenth

century realistic novel, *Dream of the Red Chamber,*[45] probably were
due more to venereal infection than to heavenly retribution. Syphilis,
on the other hand, appears to have become widespread only early in
the sixteenth century. Between 1505 and 1630, epidemics of "plum
poison" were blamed on western visitors.[46] Prostitution was first
linked with fatal disease during this era. Before the last dynasty,
prostitution may have been considered dishonorable, but it was not
regarded as unclean. By the last half of the nineteenth century, western physicians who travelled in China remarked not only on the
widespread incidence of syphilis but also on the apparent disinterest
expressed in controlling, regulating, and attempting to check the
course of the disease. Often the Chinese linked venereal disease with
the foreign community, and for this reason special prostitutes, deri-
sively called "salt water sisters,"[47] were reserved exclusively for foreigners and were prohibited from contact with the Chinese population. This appears to have been the only attempt at official control;
prostitutes otherwise were free to practice their trade even if
infected.[48]

This is not to suggest that customers and courtesans alike were
unaware of the disease or unwilling to take measures once they
suspected infection. Medical observers in the nineteenth century
remarked on the eagerness of the Chinese to self-medicate. Every
home seemed to be well stocked in basic Chinese medicines, and
when illnesses were serious or protracted, people sought out doctors, midwives, monks, and nuns for advice and medication. These
medicines, primarily vegetable and root-based and taken either as
infusions or ground into powder for pills, attempted to redress the
imbalance of the body according to ancient Chinese medical the-
ories. Venereal disease, with its symptoms of chancres and nervous-
system debilitation, was treated with only minor success by these
traditional remedies.

Medical personnel, from varied lay and religious backgrounds,
also attended to another hazard of the profession: pregnancy and
the prostitute's need to avoid childbearing. Western physicians trav-
elling to China in the nineteenth centruy were shocked to discover
blatant advertising by Chinese doctors for quick abortion. Signs
promising to "clear out the stomach," "restore virginity," or "take
out the fruit" were openly displayed on walls in city streets.[49] The
same midwives and nuns who were consulted by wives, desiring
male offspring and aphrodisiacs, seem also to have done a brisk

business in rituals and potions for birth control and abortion. Much of this was done in the name of the women's goddess, Kuan-yin, whose cult served contradictory functions; her name seems to have been invoked as much to prevent conception as to bring it on.[50] Women also turned to one another for aid; in *Daughter of Han,* an old woman provided a previously chaste widow with a preparation of garlic and crickets to induce abortion.[51]

Attempts to abort must have often proved fruitless, since brothels were staffed by natural mothers and daughters as well as those of adopted relationships. Prostitutes also suffered the ravages of too many abortions and veneral infections, and many probably became sterile. Widespread sterility among prostitutes is suggested by the frequency with which they adopted daughters to care for them in old age, and the striking lack of issue among concubines who had been obtained from houses of prostitution. The prostitutes drafted into the Imperial Household in *The Peach Blossom Fan* sang mournfully that "a peach petal blown by the breeze will never bear fruit."[52]

A more indirect, but nonetheless real, occupational danger for prostitutes was addiction. By the twentieth century prostitution seemed to westerners to be synonymous with opium, but in the nineteenth century it appears that courtesans were only occasionally addicted, although flower boats and brothels alike provided opium freely for their customers. Lower-class prostitutes, on the other hand, were heavy users of opium, and lower-level brothels usually included opium tins in each cubicle for use by both client and prostitute.[53] It is not clear from the available sources, however, just how this pattern of addiction began—via bribery by managers of lower-class brothels to keep prostitutes indebted and in line, by the ravages of opium reducing an upper-class prostitute to a lower-class brothel, or else by the widespread use of opium in all classes of brothels that, for reasons of health and economics, was more obvious in the lower-class establishments. Ironically, it seems that the most direct link between opium addiction and prostitution did not involve the prostitute's own use of the drug; rather, it was the addiction of parents, husbands, and friends, which led them to offer women for sale. There are innumerable references in literary and journalistic sources to brothel inmates sold to purchasers and procurers by their "opium sotted" husbands, brothers, fathers, uncles, and friends.[54]

In sum, then, the profession of prostitution was filled with great risk. It may have appeared to outsiders that prostitutes had their physical needs cared for in a warm, familial atmosphere, but actually they were highly susceptible to disease, physical abuse, and addiction. Only a few women could marry out or buy their freedom. The fate of the rest—courtesans and prostitutes alike—was, in the end, to be old, destitute, diseased, and discarded as "merchandise" whose desirability and livelihood had faded with their beauty.

An old folksong, translated by Florence Ayscough, a western woman who spent many years in China, described the life cycle of a courtesan, which included a terrifying portrait of old age, ordinarily regarded as a time of honor, respect, and consideration.

Mist and Flowers in Willow Lane

Mist and flowers, ah! in Willow Lane
Faces bright with harlots' rouge.
I seem among fairy maidens,
I receive official permit,
Am imposed on, wronged, by father, mother,
Who, grasping, greedy, covet silver gold;
They sell me, their slave! Tears stream,
Body is lowered, dishonored.

Aged ten and three, ten and four,
Ten and five, ten and six.
Slave is compelled to be gay,
Selected for lust, studies vice,
Ten and seven, ten and eight
I play games of forfeits, strive to please;
Lead guest to my bedroom,
Am flattered, caressed, receive money.

Don woman's skirt and hairpin,
Bright purple flowers open.
Heart takes fire,
Peony flowers open,
Study stringed instruments, singing ah!
Moon season flowers open.
Stand by to serve wine,
Fair lady flowers open.

Three-inch gold lotus feet
Lie on ivory bed;

Flowers of ecstasy bud,
Man's lust envelops me.

Gifts are bestowed, ah! silver, gold!
If gifts do not come of silver and gold,
Leathern whip descends,
Tears stream down little face.

Tears of youth may be bright Spring,
But sad, years of age, of a courtesan!
Everyone, everyone, scorns me,
Eyes of contempt regard me.

Years pass, three tens,
Am aged and worn;
Can withered flower bloom?
Old woman returns her permit.

Before bed I strum strings,
White flowers open.
Joy is hidden, gone,
Nail of Earth flowers bloom.
Everyone, everyone, loves,
Ninth Moon asters open.
Face and expression change,
Gay Ball flowers come.

Slave's family was poor—
Is indeed still poor.

Where can sons come from?
Or little girl children?
No sons can I bear,
Nor daughters beget.

For no purpose am I in Bright World,
Through Bright World walk in vain,
Enraged, resentful is Old Heaven.
Why did two words "Peach Flower"
Not drop on another?
In former life gained no merit.

Desire all day, every day,
To be led by the hand, grasped by the wrist,

Desire a pillow in common, desire to share a bed,
United behind bridal curtain.

Oh! vouchsafe this forthwith!
Moon Season Flowers do not bloom.
Incense smoke has ceased,
I am of no repute.
A heart too desperate,
Has fallen on body of slave.
Grant a fond bridegroom,
To open embroidered chamber.

Grant Heaven, for me the slave
Pray choose a young man!
Would escape, go out, from Mist Flower Lane,
Would take Heaven's Hall road.
Would follow a husband,
A husband of like mind.[55]

Sex and Eros in Chinese Society

Prostitution—registered, regulated, and relatively open—thrived
in Imperial China. Indeed, it was an integral part of a social system
that insisted on chastity and virtue from its honorable women and
restricted them to very rigid roles. The institution of prostitution was
buttressed by sexual ideology and widely held notions of eroticism.

Chinese society functioned according to a highly developed body
of beliefs in propriety, called *li*, which regulated social behavior and
granted or took away "face." There was a clear demarcation between acceptable private and public behavior, and the belief that
one area need not impinge on the other. Thus prostitutes and brothels were deemed necessary to satisfy the private needs of males
for female companionship and sex, but private activities did not
affect a man's public persona. Private life, public face, seem to have
been complementary aspects of the elite male's attitude toward
sexuality and, consequently, prostitution.

This attitude permitted an underground network of erotic and
pornographic artistic expressions even during periods of censorship
under the Ming and Ch'ing dynasties. Scholars, too, kept alive an
explicit erotic tradition concerning the prostitution quarters. These
expressions may have been prohibited as inappropriate for the *chün*

tzu (gentleman), but they were not damned as sinful. Scholars as well as officials could continue to visit the "flower gardens" and compose couplets praising the ladies of "five streets and seven lanes." Their behavior might have been punishable in theory, but it rarely was in practice. This toleration was also made possible because the higher–class sing-song girls and courtesans were directly associated with art and entertainment. The best educated courtesans, with some knowledge of the classics, could aspire to "out-scholar" the scholars, and their talents lent an aura of cultivation to the profession. It is no wonder, then, that the idealization of the sing-song girl holds so important a place in erotic literature, and her real life counterpart might aspire to an important position in the household of some scholar-official. Lower-class prostitutes benefited at least somewhat from this mystique. They were also tolerated because the Chinese state in theory, at least, traditionally provided for men's basic needs, so as not to fuel anti-establishment protest. These women could be alluded to but not explicitly described by the literati, for reasons of class bias as much as personal prestige and social propriety.

Chinese norms about sexual behavior, too, evinced a dual standard between the public and the private. Literature about sex, open discussions of sexual topics, and even vernacular fiction were all considered taboo for the public arena. Proper gentlemen and ladies were prohibited by law as well as by parental fiat from reading popular novels such as *Dream of the Red Chamber,* the late eighteenth century work which traced the romantic involvements of a young aristocrat. But a specifically erotic tradition survived clandestinely in all manner of cultural forms, including literature, sculpture, and carving.[56] Moreover, midwives and Buddhist and Taoist monks and nuns seem to have been in great demand for sexual aids and advice. The widespread practice among the elite of taking concubines was ostensibly for the purpose of producing heirs, but was also acknowledged to be for the purpose of sexual pleasure. Youths were expected to have sexual adventures, and maids in upper-class homes were often assigned to boys for sexual initiation. Immoral behavior, such as secret rendezvous of the married and unmarried alike, were far more common than elite accounts would admit. Many observers remarked that romantic love and secret trysts were immediately translated into sexual involvement in China.[57]

The relegation of sex to the most private portion of a person's life did not mean that it was deemed insignificant or unimportant. Rather, it attests to the perceived potency and power of sexual allure and behavior. The Chinese fox spirit, synonymous with erotic desire and power, was dreaded in Chinese literature and folklore and had to be appeased. Likewise, sex, and, by extension, women,[58] had to be circumscribed and privatized. The power of private needs was so great that the state had to be brought in to help supervise private morals. Indeed it was believed that in the waning years of a dynasty, there was a general deterioration in morality, and the lines between public and private behavior became blurred. Thus a new regime headed by men of clear virtue who would tighten control over society was needed.[59] This association of sexual license with dynastic weakness may have given added weight to the public supervision of private morals.

This behavior appeared hypocritical to the missionary observers of the nineteenth century. In his popular account of Chinese society, *The Middle Kingdom,* the traveller Dr. S. Wells Williams commented that "with a general regard for outward decency . . . [the Chinese] are vile and polluted in a shocking degree."[60] Western missionaries failed to comprehend the absence of sin and guilt in Confucian culture and its focus instead on appropriateness and social harmony as motivating instruments of social control.

Nowhere is the necessary bifurcation between a repressed public face and a powerful private fancy more apparent than in the great works of Chinese fiction. The women in the novel *Dream of the Red Chamber,* the play, *Romance of the Western Chamber,* and the short stories of Li Yü and others[61] are frequently powerful figures who manage their sexual weapons and their men adroitly. Faced with little choice, they often accepted the rigid sexual segregation required of women and then proceeded to manipulate and turn it to their advantage. Thus they confirm the common proverb that women should rule the home and men the world, since clearly women's power was too strong and destructive to be released. It was partly because of these restrictions placed upon women of "good" families (*liang min*), that men had such strong needs for female companionship, needs which assured the continuation of a courtesan-prostitute tradition. Women's power, and its accompanying force of sexual energy, which had to be regulated and restricted, was symbolized in the common literary image of the cruel, scheming concubine. This image has a long tradition in Chinese literature.

The decadent secondary wife is the real villain of *Golden Lotus,* a tale set at the end of the Ming and widely read in the Ch'ing. Here, the unleashed power of a woman not only brought down a great house but implicitly was responsible for the fall of a great empire as well.

CHAPTER TWO: LAW, *LI*, AND POPULAR MENTALITY

Prostitution flourished in urban society in late Imperial times. Although this was still a society that placed great emphasis on female virtue and seclusion, parents, husbands, and relatives regularly sold their offspring, wives, and relatives into prostitution. Thus, if we are to understand this institution and the condition of women in Chinese society, we must examine the perceptions that underlay the sellers' attitudes. Before we explore economic considerations, we must first look at the legal and moral context within which Chinese families operated.

Prostitution in Law and Li

In the traditions of Confucianism and Legalism, China developed two very different approaches to political philosophy. Confucianists adhered to the belief that the ideal society could be reached only when people knew and behaved in ways appropriate to their different stations in life. Men and women had clearly differentiated roles, whether they were noble or humble, superior or inferior. Within the family, further distinctions were drawn by generation, age, degree of relationship, and sex. These differences were as important to Confucianists as those in the larger society. A complex set of notions about appropriate behavior for each station, known as *li*, had evolved. *Li* can be roughly translated as "propriety" or, more specifically, as "rules of behavior varying in accordance with one's status defined in the various forms of social relationships."[1] Legalists, on the other hand, considered the differences among people in society irrelevant and believed that the ideal society could only be realized if legal and political order were maintained through the use of orders, punishments, and rewards. They insisted on objective, absolute standards of behavior for all subjects, regardless of status.

By late Ming and Ch'ing times, these two traditions had become so interwoven that the law codes, a Legalist instrument, were largely "Confucianized." The codes were replete with differentiations and sanctions according to social rank and family position. They provided punishments for offenses such as murder, theft, and injury and prescribed behavioral norms for celebrations, festivals, and rituals. The code included sumptuary regulations for clothing, food, housing, and transportation.[2]

Ch'ing statutes (*lü*) were an amalgam of laws handed down from earlier codes, those newly promulgated by imperial edicts, and proposals by officials approved by the throne. Precedents, also important, were incorporated at regular intervals into the codes.[3] The sources of *li*, however, are less obvious. The most important guides to behavior were the classics that formed the basis of the education of the elite. Their notions were disseminated to the masses through popular morality books and a system of local lectures on morality ordered by imperial mandate. Other sources of *li* seem to have been local or regional customs, practiced long and widely enough to be recognized as expected behavior, and therefore elevated to the status of conventional morality.[4]

However, we cannot speak only of law and *li* as the sole determinants of morality. The official and gentry elite were often remiss in their responsibilities to "educate" the people in appropriate law and *li*. The populace often had only a vague notion of the complexity of the actual codes and followed their local customs instead. Since customs varied widely—the Chinese proverbially say that "customs change evey ten miles"—discrepancies always existed between local behavior and the laws, rules, and regulations recognized and enforced by the national elite. Therefore, when discussing the sociolegal standing of prostitution in Chinese society, one must differentiate at least two kinds of standards: law and *li* on the one hand, and local attitudes and beliefs that often formed a separate standard of morality on the other.[5]

Prostitution was never condemned by statute in Ch'ing China. The only prohibitions were against civil and military officials visiting brothels. Instead, it was permitted, regulated, and taxed. Prostitution was made available for the satisfaction of male demands for sex and companionship and to produce revenue for the civil authorities. Some of the statutes and administrative regulations relevant to prostitution can be found in collected codes of the empire. Many others, however, were local regulations and precedents that established special districts for the pleasure quarters and set taxing and licensing procedures. Since those were acts by separate municipalities, they are much less accessible to western scholars today. Portions of later Ch'ing codes are available, however, and statutes relevant to prostitution are found in the areas that regulate the registration of the population, the treatment of stray children, marriage, and incest and adultery.[6]

The entire Chinese population had to be registered with local authorities. This registration included the listing of occupation and thus aided taxation as well as social control.[7] The practice of posting prostitutes' names outside their *ch'ing lou* (brothels) undoubtedly served the purpose of registration as well as advertisement. The removal of a woman's name from the lists as a prostitute was a necessary, and frequently expensive, prerequisite to making her a primary or secondary wife.

The second area of the code that indirectly concerned prostitution was the section on the treatment of "stray" children and slaves. Harsh punishments were prescribed for those who sold strayed, lost, or fugitive children, or slaves, into marriage. These children or slaves were to be returned to their families or owners.[8] The females covered by this statute—orphans wandering in cities and famine areas, mistreated young concubines and brides, and juvenile adopted daughters-in-law who had run away—were a ready supply for "sellers of the flesh."

The third set of statutes relevant to prostitution were those concerning marriage. Statutes expressly forbade the hiring out of wives and daughters (probably a practice similar to the pawning mentioned in several sources), the taking in marriage by force of a free man's wife or daughter, the marriage of officials and clerks to musicians or comedians, and marriage between free people and slaves.[9] Again, these statutes underscore that it was necessary for a prostitute or courtesan to leave her profession if she were to marry and be admitted to respectable society.

Lastly, in the section "Incest and Adultery," intercourse between servants and their owners' wives or daughters, and between officers of the government and prostitutes or actresses was deemed criminal.[10] The punishment for officials—sixty blows or one degree of degradation—was rather severe, but appears to have had little deterrent effect and probably was not enforced very often.

The legal code of the empire, however, was not very concerned with prostitutes. Its interest was in developing good officials, guiding and protecting women of good families, and maintaining clear distinctions between the various strata in society. Most of the statutes and precedents concerning prostitution were established by local governments, such as the system promulgated in Shanghai in 1877. These laws called for the registration of brothels, the licensing of prostitutes, health examinations for prostitutes, and the establishment of special hospitals for those who were diseased.[11]

When we turn from law to *li*, we see that prostitution, although legal, continued to be condemned in conventional morality. Since Confucianism's redefinition during the late T'ang (618—907) and Sung dynasty (960—1279), women had been restricted and limited to a narrow role within the family.[12] The ideal, attainable only by those with wealth and education, relegated women to virtual purdah in the private women's quarters of the home. Training in thought and behavior was just as important for this segregated life as the teaching of domestic skills. Texts were created explicitly for the purpose of transmitting the ideals of *li*. The *Nü erh ching* (*Classics for Girls*) and the *Lieh nü chuan* (*Biographies of Famous Women*) were virtually required reading for parents and daughters. From these biographies it appears that appropriate *li* for women was much less class defined than for men; what did differentiate women was their ability to realize these ideals.

A biographical entry in an abridged version of the *Lieh nü chuan*, called the *Kuei fan*, demonstrates the emphasis placed on chastity for young maidens. In the story of the Washing Silk Woman, a woman who had never before spoken to a man committed suicide after a young soldier stopped to ask for some food and directions. His innocent questioning gave her no choice but to jump into the river.[13] Biographies were also included in official local histories. Sections entitled "Honorable and Virtuous Women" were meant to instill correct attitudes toward husbands, as well as chastity, courage, tenacity, and unquestioning acceptance of the prevailing hierarchies unto death. Indeed, fifteen of the fifty-six women in one such history had committed suicide.[14] The popular stories of the mother of the philosopher Mencius, who continually sacrificed herself to insure her son's future success as a scholar, highlight the domestic sphere and strict standards appropriate for women.[15] These local histories also included biographies of widows of determination and strict moral purpose. A widow in Shantung province, who survived until age eighty-one, raised her own son, the two sons of her husband's first wife, and one orphaned grandson, all of whom became successful examination candidates.[16] Clearly, these ideals would condemn, not console, the poor daughter or wife sold into prostitution.

Prostitutes as Legal "Mean" People

Since society was clearly differentiated by rank, and status was clearly correlated with income and education, a notion of class was inherent in law. Indeed, since ancient times there had been three legal classes—official, commoner, and mean (*chien min*). The last category included prostitutes.[17] Transgressions of the law were punished according to the class of the criminal as well as of the victim. Good government required that people be instructed in the social and legal differences between them and behave accordingly.

Most people belonged to the great middle category of commoner. Some authors have estimated that even by late Ch'ing, when the ranks of officialdom were swollen, the scholar-official class never accounted for more than 1.3 percent of the total population.[18] People classified as "mean" were also a small fraction of the total population, perhaps less than 1 percent, although in some regions the proportion might have been higher. The mean category, originally intended for punishment and social control, included conquered minority groups, subjects punished for remaining loyal to a previous dynasty, slaves, and certain groups, such as those whose occupations took them away from their ancestral homes—government runners, barbers, peddlers, actors, and prostitutes. Classification as mean meant registration separate from commoners, and mean people and their descendants were prohibited from marrying commoners or participating in government examinations. Cut off from normal avenues of mobility and expected to fulfill certain occupational roles, they formed a separate caste.[19]

But the classification had undergone changes by late Imperial times. Successive imperial decrees during the Ch'ing had manumitted most hereditary groups formerly classified as mean, with the proviso that the next three generations not engage in mean occupations. But given the lack of other occupations and of social mobility, many had no choice but to continue in mean occupations. Even those who did enter new occupations suffered discrimination well into the twentieth century, despite imperial decrees. The most important result, for our purposes, was that certain occupations for women continued to be linked with this caste, such as hairdressing, footbinding, midwifery, matchmaking, attending brides, peddling women's trinkets, and procuring. Many poor female commoners, especially those destitute and alone in cities with no familial support, also entered these mean occupations. In late Imperial times, therefore, the hereditary nature of meanness had broken down as commoners, out of economic necessity, entered traditionally mean occupations, while the legal basis of hereditary mean groups was eroded.

Prostitutes constituted a special case among the *chien min*. Some were young women who were mean be dint of their families' classifiction. Since *chien min* were not thought to know *li*, and were often poor and unskilled, they had very little occupational choice. These women were prostitutes because they were mean; they were women against whom the prohibitions concerning marriage and mobility for descendants were strictly enforced.[20]

Other women—those born free but sold or pawned into prostitution and those few who had chosen the profession—were legally required to register as prostitutes, a mean occupation. In contrast to women born to meanness, they became mean when they became prostitutes. Although by definition mean, they were freer to leave the category if they were able to marry or to purchase their freedom.[21] Accounts of the purchase of prostitutes often refer to the necessity of changing these women's registration. The story "From Rags to Riches" tells of the large sum of money (3,000 ounces of silver) needed to take women out of prostitution, since the madam had to be both reimbursed for her loss and bribed to remove the name from the registers.[22] But only a small minority of women were able to leave the profession, and for most, the mean classification they had acquired was just as permanent as if they had been born into it. It was only a small consolation for them that the category had lost much of its legal force by the late Ch'ing; the social opprobrium remained and probably affected most stringently those women who had entered prostitution out of economic necessity.

There is evidence that the public, attuned to caste distinctions, recognized a déclassé category long after the legal justifications for it had disappeared. An anecdote by the narrator of *Vignettes* tells of an academic who was demoted after committing an imprudent act.

> "Where would he be after this five rank demotion" I asked. "What is there left?" Chi-chih asked. "The first degradation would lower him to the eight rank . . . the second to the ninth, the third to unclassified, the fourth to the position of a common subject and the fifth—oh god—there is nothing worse. Oh yes, there are prostitutes, actors, servants, and coolies. Therefore the five degradations would make him a prostitute!" "But there are no male prostitutes," Chi-chih said. "Then he would be a brothel keeper," I answered."[23]

Clearly, not only did a notion of déclassé still exist by late Ch'ing times, but this category had become synonymous with disreputable and immoral occupations in which one could not be expected to be well versed in *li*.

Prostitutes as Legal Slaves

More significant for prostitutes than their mean classification was the fact that many—some observers suggested as high as 80 percent—were slaves.[24] The mean category often tended to be a legal fiction; the slave designation, on the other hand, was legal and economic fact. Although slavery was made illegal in 1906, there were no real efforts to abolish it until the 1930s. Legal distinctions existed between three kinds of people in servitude—permanent slaves, hired servants, and pawned or bond servants—although they were often confused in practice. The hired servant, *yung kung,* was an independent man or woman whose services, normally for domestic work, were contracted by a master. Hired servants received a definite wage and usually worked for an agreed-upon amount of time, after which they were free to leave. During their period of service they were practically family members, yet certain distances were maintained. The relationship could end with the completion of service, although instances abound of servants remaining indefinitely with families.

Pawned or bond servants were also legally free. These were people who had pawned themselves, or, more frequently, were women who had been pawned by husbands or parents. Pawning carried with it a guaranteed length of tenure, after which redemption could be made. If a pawned servant stayed longer and was given a husband or wife by the employer, the rupture was less easy to make. In fact, servants pawned for a period of less than three years who had not been given mates were equated with hired labor by Ch'ing law. Those of tenure over three years who had been given partners were considered slaves.[25]

By contrast, slaves (*nu p'u,* males, and *nu pei,* females) were both mean people and legal non-persons. True chattels,[26] private slaves were considered on a par with material possessions, and masters had nearly total control over them. Slave status was hereditary and marriages of slaves were arranged by the owners, sometimes with slaves of the same household but more often between slaves of different households. Generally, male slaves remained in the houshold for life and female slaves left upon marriage, although female slaves who had borne the master's children often remained in the household as concubines.

Most Chinese slaves were used for domestic work. Retinues of domestic slaves served an important role as symbols of conspicuous consumption in well-to-do families. This was recognized by sumptuary laws, which always included regulations on the permissible numbers of slaves.[27] Slaves had to be taken care of for a much longer time than hired servants, and the responsibilitites of the family toward them were much broader. Thus slavery flourished in China when wealthy families could afford to increase their households with these symbols of wealth and when the supply of potential women for slaves was high and could permit careful selection. Both of these conditions were met in late Ch'ing times.

The link between prostitution and slavery was usually indirect in the late Ch'ing period. Generally girls and young women were first sold into domestic slavery, either directly by relatives or through middlemen. They would be brought into a family to work for a portion of their childhood, adolescence, and perhaps early womanhood. If the family's fortunes declined, and if a slave was attractive, she might then be resold to a brothel or into one of the procuring networks that led into a brothel. This resale, although expressly forbidden by Ch'ing law, was widely practiced and usually quite profitable. Meanwhile, the family had benefited from the woman's labor. After purchase by a brothel, the prostitute retained her slave status, regaining freedom only if purchased by a husband. Some women who had been pawned and then traded into prostitution could certainly hope for eventual redemption, but freedom for them was just as remote as for the slave, and their status was soon indistinguishable from that of slaves. They were usually deprived of the chance to redeem themselves by managers who encouraged indebtedness until there was no longer a chance of reimbursement.

All slave women were the property of their masters, who held absolute rights over their persons and whose only responsibility was for their basic care. In cases of maltreatment, deception, or trickery, slaves, who were legal non-persons and therefore could not bring suit, had no recourse in law. Their only hope was for a commoner to intercede for them, which was unlikely since public defense of a prostitute would make one disreputable.[28]

Foreign observers, especially reforming zealots such as Elizabeth Andrews in the late nineteenth century and Mrs. Hazelwood in the early twentieth, noted the increasing connection between slavery and the trade in adopted daughters. Indeed the two became almost synonymous in the 1920s and 1930s as people avoided the growing legal and social stigma attached to slavery. Even in the nineteenth century, however, slave owners employed the legal fiction of "adopted daughter." Rather than purchasing a woman or girl child outright as they had in the past, they either deceived parents into believing they were adopting their daughters, when they were not, or they adopted the girls and then exploited them as servants. Apparently, both the ignorance and desperation of the parents contributed to these illegal acts. In the 1870s a group of missionary women in Hong Kong and South China tried to bring the widespread abuse of the adopted daughter system, and its frequent connection with the traffic in women and children, to the British Crown's attention. But the adopted daughter institution proved remarkably impervious to reform, especially since the young women themselves were unable to testify in a court of law. A number of fictionalized accounts in the nineteenth and early twentieth centuries, such as *Travels of Lao Ts'an,* and *The Third Daughter* took the adopted daughters' perspective, describing how the power of the master coupled with a young woman's vulnerability left no alternative but compliance.[29]

Prostitution and Popular Mentality

Prostitutes were legally non-persons and were officially considered mean. Yet there is evidence that within the more fluid, changeable realm of local custom, attitudes towards them, as towards other sexually active women, were ambiguous and often not quite as harsh. Old Lady Ning's neighbors in *Daughter of Han* encouraged her to make her living as a prostitute when her husband spent all the family money on opium.[30] Many folk ballads present sexually active women in an accepting light,[31] and novels and short stories from the late Ch'ing are replete with women who defy the constraints of *li*. Indeed sexually active nuns and widows are common characters in the literature.[32] Significantly, in these sources, prostitutes are regarded as motivated by economic necessity rather than by sexual desire. This is not to deny that moral reprobation existed. Strong disapproval of both prostitution and sexually loose women was expressed by popular religion, especially in the morality pamphlets, *shan shu,* describing the passage through Hell. These tracts, produced by barely literate priests, schoolteachers, and unemployed scholars, were frequently Buddhist-inspired and drew heavily on folk religion and a popularized, simplified Confucianism. By the late Ch'ing they tended to present a narrow, puritanical vision of women, recounting gruesome tortures in Hell for adultresses, abortionists, and prostitutes, and soundly condemning those who sold others into prostitution.[33]

In vernacular literature, however, the innocent women sold into slavery and prostitution by greedy relatives or desperate parents are not portrayed as thoroughly debased creatures. Instead, like the two sisters in *Travels of Lao Ts'an,* they are women who somehow managed, while "making their bed on dew and feeding on air," to remain chaste in spirit if not in fact.[34] More often than not, as soon as the women in these stories find men to redeem them, they are immediately transformed into faithful wives, content to be cared for and secluded. (It was even commonly believed that prostitutes, having already lived a loose life, made better wives and concubines than women who had always been secluded and who therefore might be more prone to temptation.) This magical transformation required only that women believe and behave according to the clear-cut standards of *li*.

In sum, the image of prostitutes in the popular mentality was complex. Condemned and restricted by well-known, if frequently misunderstood, notions of law and *li*, the prostitute could be redeemed if she bore herself in all other ways as a woman of virtue and longed for a husband and sons. In fact, many celebrated courtesans-concubines, such as Tung Hsiao-wan, concubine of the famous

Ch'ing scholar Mao P'i-chiang,[35] were destined to be both married and happy. Of course the courtesan stood a much better chance than the lower class prostitute of being eventually transformed into a "good" woman. She could use her familiarity with the classics and her greater wealth and higher status to present herself as an artist. But lower-class prostitutes had neither the opportunity for real education nor the income to afford the accoutrements of culture.

The difference was not between good and bad women. Instead, courtesans and good women were separated by a short distance on one end of a continuum, and lower-class prostitutes were clustered on the other end. In the final analysis, it was class that gave good women and courtesans more commonality than profession denied, and it was class that proved an almost inpenetrable barrier to the lower-class harlot. As we shall see, the destruction of the courtesans' self-definition as artists and the decline in their status in popular culture in the twentieth century was a blow to those songstresses whose higher status had been their only protection from total degradation.

CHAPTER THREE: SEXUAL ECONOMY

The sale of women for prostitution was only an extreme form of the general trade in women which included the adoption of daughters and future daughters-in-law, and the purchase of servants and of brides. Common to all these transactions was the possibility that a woman might subsequently be resold into prostitution. Parents (and the women themselves) may have regarded some fates as preferable to others, but the brisk trade in women for prostitution occurred in a unique context in which a thriving market in women already existed and all women were to some extent regarded as merchandise. One has only to read accounts of marriages—both real and fictionalized—particularly in poorer families, to note the startling frequency with which fathers spoke about "buying a bride" for their sons or "selling their daughters" as brides.[1]

The most blatant forms of this exchange in women were usually linked with economic deprivation, either real or anticipated, but in all classes women were regarded as objects to be invested in or bartered. Even daughters of upper-class families were considered luxury items to be indulged in or expended, depending upon the economic health and social prestige of the family. While families may also have regarded sons as economic investments, unlike daughters, they were not usually considered disposable. It was women's fate to be separated from their families, but all families held onto the fiction if not always the fact of keeping sons under one roof and around one stove.

Women's Fate

China has always appeared to be a child-oriented society which indulged infants and young children until the age of six or seven. Yet, the birth of a girl was often considered unfortunate,[2] since it granted no prestige to the mother and gave no assurance that filial duties would be discharged. Western missionaries, obsessed with distinguishing the "civilized" from the "barbaric," frequently recorded invidious proverbs about girl children, such as "one deformed son is worth a daughter as wise as the eighteen Lohans," or "a boy is worth ten girls."[3]

Missionary sources also contain an extensive debate on the topic of infanticide,[4] although it is difficult to determine the degree to which it was actually practiced. The persistence of reports, the admission by parents and midwives that daughters were not permitted to live, and local and provincial government proclamations against the practice[5] all argue that the custom did in fact exist, although perhaps more in the South than in the North. Infanticide increased, moreover, in times of real or anticipated hardship and distress. The Dutch Dr. Schlegel quoted an often repeated proverb that "it is better to kill the body than the soul."[6] Far more female than male souls, however, seem to have been rendered this mercy.

Female infanticide was tolerated under certain extreme conditions. Girls—like seedlings and savings—were considered expendable by those who lived on the margin of subsistence. For many parents, irrespective of social class, female children represented a net drain on the family economy that offered no future compensation in filial duties. Girls, therefore, could expect less attention, food, and affection from their families. Viewed from this perspective, female infanticide was an extreme manifestation of the economically rational predispositon of Chinese families in late Imperial times to place less importance on keeping girl children. The devaluation of females was in part the result of the later separation of a girl from her family by marriage, and tended to pave the way for other kinds of ruptures, such as sale or pawning.

The ideal of a carefree girlhood was only attained in the most comfortable households. Autobiographies of well-to-do women,[7] as well as novels such as *Dream of the Red Chamber,* recount days of carefree play, but for children of the poorer classes, especially females, childhood was not a time of indulgence. When mothers in rural areas worked, children often accompanied them on their backs. Urban women, like Old Lady Ning in *Daughter of Han,* had to find someone to care for their children. In the poorest families, young children worked at home as soon as they could walk or were sent out to work if employment was available.[8]

When times were' hard, moreover, girls risked being separated from families by death, sale, pawning, or adoption. Adoption, which freed the natal family from the necessity of supporting the daughter while giving the adopting family the use of the girl's services, was popular among lower classes. It took two distinct forms: adoption as a future daughter-in-law, *yang hsi* (or Cantonese *sim-pua*), which was considered a betrothal, and adoption as a real daughter, *yang nü,* literally, a "girl who is raised."[9] In the case of the *yang hsi,* the girl became a part of the family, as would any daughter-in-law, retaining her maiden name and ties with her natal family, and able to visit them several times a year. Disposal of a prospective daughter-in-law legally required the consent of the natal family and involved the routine procedure for dissolving a betrothal. In adoption as a *yang nü,* a real daughter, the girl severed all ties with her natal family, took the adopting family's surname, and was considered by the adopting family as a natural daughter. Disposal of a *yang nü* by sale, marriage, or further adoption required no consultation with the natal family. The two forms of adoption were further complicated by the common practice of adopting a prospective daughter-in-law when a family had no sons, often in the belief that girls "summoned younger brothers"(*chao hsiao ti*), that is, encouraged the foster mother to give birth to sons. There were, in addition, a host of other less honorable practices, such as adopting an older daughter-in-law, intended for a much younger boy, to work in the house and perhaps even care for her child husband-to-be, or adopting a daughter-in-law for a hopelessly crippled, retarded, or otherwise infirm son and for her labor as well.

There seems to have been a great deal of ambiguity and confusion concerning the forms of adoption. Western observers were often unaware of any distinctions and referred only to "adopted daughters" (or, in the South, *mui tsai*).[10] Some Chinese parents and adopting families seem purposely to have perpetuated the confusion, and others simply did not understand that there were legal distinctions between the forms of adoption and sale. For example, in the few surviving missionary copies of contracts for the transfer of girl children, parents usually surrendered total control of their children.[11] The transfers were therefore actually *yang nü* adoptions or slave purchases, although, in many cases, there may have been verbal understandings that these were adoptions for early betrothal. Since a slave or servant cost more than an adopted daughter-in-law (the former involving a transfer of ownership), it was in the economic interest of the purchaser to disguise all transactions as the cheaper *yang hsi* adoption procedure. Parents, perhaps erroneously, believed that an adopted daughter stood a better chance of good

treatment than a servant or slave and thus were more easily convinced to part with daughters for adoption and early betrothal. A
sale into prostitution was generally regarded with dismay, and few
parents would openly consent to it. Adoption was the most frequent
ruse employed by procurers.[12]

Motivations for exopting daughters were as complex as those for
adopting girls. Poorer families preferred to exopt rather than raise
daughters who were economically unprofitable. Adopting families
preferred early betrothal because it was cheaper than "buying a
bride" later, gave them the girl's labor for a number of years, and
tended to reduce tension between mothers- and daughters-in-law.
Families of all classes exopted for any number of superstitious reasons, such as blaming a daughter for a family misfortune. But the
motives most commonly cited were economic; females represented a
drain on family resources.[13]

In the twentieth century, the League of Nations and the world
community expressed concern over the international traffic in
women, but they overlooked the far more prevalent internal circula-
tion of girls and young women in rural and urban areas of China.
This was such a thriving market that in many communities a female
child from a poor home stood little chance of escaping a sale or
trade of some kind and passing her entire childhood with her natal
family. The most sobering fact, however, was not that these transactions regularly occurred, but that they often were repeated many
times during a woman's life.[14]

By the age of six or seven, girls began serious preparations for
womanhood. In less well-to-do families, this usually entailed household duties, outdoor farm work in those rural areas where women
were allowed to work in the fields, or employment outside the
home. Girls in most wealthy households were taught finer "feminine" skills, although a minority were given an education similar to
males.[15]

Except for girls of the poorest families and certain minorities, the
preparation for womanhood was symbolized by the deliberate dis-
tortion of the feet by footbinding.[16] Women of the lower classes
were not expected to attain the three inch "lilies" so admired in
their upper-class counterparts, but the increasingly tight binding and
accompanying pain were theirs as well. Erotic novels and descriptions of famous beauties, especially higher-class courtesans, always
included references to the size, shape, and fragrance of the little

"orchid hooks."[17] Lower-class prostitutes were sometimes ridiculed as "yellow fish"—women with natural feet.[18] The size of the deformed foot was often a crucial variable in marriage transactions; one missionary reported that the question most asked of the prospective bride was not about her beauty but about the size of her feet.[19] Beauty was heaven-sent, it was reasoned, but footbinding directly reflected parental wishes and control. The practice of footbinding, which existed for nearly a thousand years in China, was sign and a symbol of women's position.

With her feet bound, trained in household skills, and socialized in the four feminine virtues of right behavior, proper speech, proper demeanor, and proper employment, a woman was ready for marriage between the ages of thirteen and fifteen, if she had not already been exopted, sold, or pawned by her parents. The parents, after choosing a go-between (usually an older woman in the community known for matchmaking success), made it known that the girl was in the marriage market. The ensuing negotiations often involved intricate maneuvering by the majority of families who had considerable "face" to win or lose by the matches made for their children. Poorer families had fewer options, and the poorest often had to settle for socially less than ideal arrangements, such as concubinage, uxorilocal marriages, or marriages to widowers, criminals, or the infirm.[20]

According to foreign observers, the phenomenon of single women without husbands of some sort was singularly absent from China. There were societies of female "abstinents," usually around Buddhist women's houses, but these were so rare they were considered a most bizarre anomaly in Chinese society.[21] Most families were able to dispose of daughters: by marriage as an adult or by the less preferable sale or adoption as a young girl, which left others to take of the decisions of womanhood.

That almost all women were eventually spoken for was not necessarily a source of great pleasure for the women themselves. The rite of marriage was almost universally regarded as a sad occasion, since the status and security of a wife upon first entering her husband's home were the lowest in her life. Married to a man she usually had never seen, cut off from her natal family except on certain ritualized occasions, separated from family and childhood friends by long distances due to strict exogamous rules, a new wife had virtually no one on whom to rely. She was really a servant for her mother-in-law, and even her husband could not have been counted on as an ally since, according to the Chinese proverb, he had "not married a wife but a daughter-in-law."[22] In early disputes he was more likely to keep family peace by siding with his mother. She was either a potential threat or virtually a non-person to other family members who addressed her not by name, but by her relationship to her husband. It was only by being hardworking and compliant and, more importantly, by quickly bearing a son that she could begin to build up a power base within the larger household. For most women, any later success came at the expense of many servile and frequently miserable years.

For most women of the upper classes, this stage of life meant comfort, but also required virtual seclusion. From puberty women were regarded "as dangerous as smuggled salt," and married women were locked within the walls of the women's quarters. They were allowed to leave only rarely—for occasional visits to family and friends, to go on a pilgrimage, or to attend a festival. Women of the lower classes had harsher lives with more physical labor, but at least they had more freedom of movement and were able to go outside the family compound for farm work or marketing. Yet peasant women in the more conservative North were restricted in their outdoor farm work and confined as closely as possible to the home. Old Lady Ning recounted how poor village women looked out from behind compound walls, venturing beyond only with their faces covered. It was not uncommon for young women to wish that they might be born in the next life as dogs, in order to be free to wander around.[23]

Women who were able to surmount all these obstacles and become strong and aggressive were often derogatorily called shrews, *p'o fu,* or women who "reviled the streets" to such a degree that "people do not know east from west" and "men are worn out and horses exhausted," and even "the mountains tremble and the earth shakes."[24] Many women, though, were not blessed with such powers or with sons. For them, as Old Lady Ning complained, life indeed was "not auspicious."[25] Divorce, although possible in law, was rare, and then usually only at the husband's initiative. Only under the most extreme situations, such as severe physical abuse, could women bring suit for divorce.[26]

A few women were able to leave their husband's homes. Concubines ran away, wives deserted with lovers, and, most commonly, women turned to their natal families for protection against abusive husbands or in-laws. Old Lady Ning returned to her family for nearly half of every month while her parents were still living.[27] But women who left their husbands paid a high price. They usually had to surrender their children, particularly sons, to their husband's family. In a society that placed a heavy emphasis on roots, they faced an uncertain existence, and, if they had run away, usually capture and remorse. Some women opted to leave in other ways; fits of crazed behavior, often interpreted as spirit possession, permitted women at least a psychological retreat when burdens or tragedies became overwhelming. The high incidence of suicide among young women fifteen to twenty-four was also a very real form of escape from successive sales and miserable marriages. This desperate act revealed not only the dearth of other options but also an inherent hostility and desire for revenge, since the Chinese believed that suicide released a "hungry ghost" to wreak havoc on those responsible unless it was appeased and expiated.[28]

If a woman survived her mother-in-law's tyranny, perhaps a half dozen childbirths aided by midwives of uneven competence, a lifetime of economic fluctuations, and had been fortunate enough to bear sons, she could face old age with relative security and equanimity. But so happy an ending was far from certain—or the norm. "Give heed to the voice of an old woman; sorrow has given her wisdom" is an old saying.[29] Old Lady Ning's life encompassed the Great North China Famine of 1876-79, the sale of her daughters, reduction to penury by her "opium sot" of a husband, begging, and stints of employment as a servant. However, her old age was made respectable and secure because a son, born late in life, provided her with a home and grandchildren. Of course, a secure position was more likely for those with wealth. In fact, elder women in official households, like the grandmother in *Dream of the Red Chamber,* virtually ran the entire family economy, managing the intricate relationships between family members, concubines, and servants as well as the complex household routine.

Women without husbands or families to support them in their old age were in extremely precarious situations. "A good girl never marries twice," women were told, and a widow expected to remain in her husband's household and be supported. But she often found herself pressured by his relatives to remarry since, according to the Ch'ing Legal Code, the wife's dowry and her husband's property could then revert to his family.[30] Sometimes, widows were sold as slaves, servants, or prostitutes.

Only a few jobs, low in pay and status, were available to these women. They included peddling food and trinkets, sewing, a few positions in orphanages and asylums, jobs as nurses, child companions, houseworkers, maids, servants in convents, and the lowest servants in gambling houses, teahouses, brothels, and post stations.[31] Old Lady Ning recorded one tale after another of older women with no recourse but to beg or be involved in questionable occupations; one woman was reduced to begging when her daughter moved away after selling all her mother's belongings, including the eyeglasses necessary for her sewing.[32]

Charitable institutions for the care of the elderly poor were practically non-existent. Missionaries, coming from a strong tradition of private rather than public charity, were appalled at the apparent lack of benevolence among the Chinese. Unaware that the Chinese state had traditionally been more involved than any western nation in caring for people in distress, they did not realize that traditional forms of relief had disintegrated or been exhausted by the late nineteenth century.[33] In their search for private acts and asylums, all that they could find were a few public spirited individuals, some traditional Buddhist almsgiving, some distribution of free clothing and foodstuffs, and a limited number of institutions for the aged, abandoned, infirm, and destitute. But the reason for the lack of public or private charitable institutions for women goes deeper than the disintegration of government services in the late nineteenth century.

To the Chinese male, men existed as part of the great chain, linking home to the state. Just as *yin* had become subordinate to *yang,* women had become appendages to men, necessary to continue the life line but never regarded apart from it. The obligation for their care was totally with the family, not the state. The exceptions served to reinforce these views; a few women widowed for twenty to thirty years were designated as "chaste" and given state pensions to help them serve as models for all women.[34] The old woman in *Daughter of Han* whose daughter had stolen her eyeglasses finally attempted suicide by jumping off a bridge. Her attempt was unsuccessful and her suffering body became a town spectacle. No one apparently thought of individual rescue or relief.[35]

This lack of public care and responsibility for women without families was the complement of the position of women within families, and helps explain the brothel's fictive familial relationships and prostitutes' unending search for husbands. Men had opportunities, at least in theory, to leave the home and be defined apart from it. Women had no such alternative; their sole definition was familial.

Some of the occupations available to older women, such as sewing, servant work, and peddling, gave them access to the segregated women's quarters of wealthier households. Many used this privileged access to become involved in procuring, an occupation which could provide a comfortable income. Sometimes, they procured by subtle manipulation; the famous concubine Sai Chin-hua was transformed into a sing-song girl by the older women entrusted to her footbinding.[36] Other times, they engaged in forceful abduction; the older women who acted as go-betweens, peddlers, and hairdressers in *Golden Lotus, Dream of the Red Chamber,* and other novels, plotted to kidnap attractive, innocent young women.

Thus, the involvement of older women in procuring forced women to come full circle: sold by parents for economic gain, women were often destined to become sellers or procurers of young women when they were no longer beautiful and had no other options. Old women often had little recourse but to turn upon other women for their survival, whether it be mother-in-law on daughter-in-law, daughters-in-law on other daughters-in-law, or older women procuring younger for sale and servitude. In late Imperial times, economic realities forced many women into a metaphorical cannibalism—women were forced to feed upon the young of their sex.

The Wages of Famine

The relationship in China between the sale of women and fluctuations in the economy was particularly clear during times of famine. Informal networks for the sale of women always operated in cities and local market centers where there were poor, destitute, or simply unwanted women and children. But in times of famine, this normally clandestine operation went public. Missionaries in the nineteenth century could quickly surmise the economic health of an area by the percentage of families that still contained husband, wife, and children, especially girl children.[37] Famines occurred frequently during the period for which we have adequate records, with at least one province being affected nearly every year.[38] The Great North China Famine of 1876-79 was particularly devastating.[39]

By the autumn of 1876, the famine had spread to the five northernmost provinces, with Shansi and its population of fifteen million

the most severely ravaged. "That people pull down their houses, sell
their wives and daughters, eat roots and carrion, clay and refuse, is
news which nobody wonders at. It is the regular thing," wrote a
Baptist missionary, Timothy Richards.[40] When the worst of the famine was over in 1880, Shansi's governor estimated that 80 percent of
the population had experienced extreme privation, and that at least
nine and one half million people had died,[41] a figure roughly compa-
rable to the number of all military deaths in World War I.

The Traffic in Women

It would appear that in situations such as the Great North China
Famine, the Chinese generally surrendered first their savings, seed,
and "luxury" items, next their draft animals, then their farm tools
and implements, and, finally, their private household possessions,
family members, and house land and timber. One barely credible
report from a hard-hit Shansi district tells of over 100,000 women
and children sold.[42] Missionaries everywhere noted the absence of
women and children, one writing in 1877 that "in many places sel-
dom are to be seen any women, especially young ones. In a
village . . . where I went . . . all the women except two very old
ones and all the children of both sexes had been sold."[43] Sometimes,
there were not enough buyers, and children had to be killed or
abandoned. In orphanages established by missionaries, abandoned
girls outnumbered boys by as much as two to one.[44] Despite the
good intentions of the missionaries, the mortality rate in these institutions was inordinately high. Sale was clearly the preferable course
for both parents and children.

Many sales resembled the slave auctions of antebellum America.
Sometimes, perhaps in areas under close official supervision, the
trade was carried on clandestinely in private homes to which families or middlemen brought girls to be sold to dealers. Dr. Richards
recounted that a woman in Shansi invited him to go into a nearby
house because "there are all young girls there wanting to be taken
away."[45] Frequently, however, sales and resales took place on the
auction block; Dr. Richards recalled one harrowing night

> "in a village inn among the mountains of . . . Shantung . . .
> where a market for the sale of women was going on, attended
> by men who had come from the Far East to buy. I slept little

that night because of the great commotion and distress. The
women who hadn't been bought were imploring to be taken
away, anyhow, even for nothing, rather than be left to perish
of starvation . . . ."[46]

The extent of this trade was enormous. Missionaries like Richards reported "meeting carts daily full of women being taken away
for sale." A magistrate in Szechuan convicted of slave running had
several times landed boatloads of women for profitable resale.[47]
Famine areas attracted speculators from all over China, including
small time soldiers, unemployed city folk, local ruffians, bandit
gangs, local officials, and military officers.

Only a hazy outline of this network can be discerned from our
sources, and we can only begin to appreciate the vicious cycle begun
by this trade. The siphoning off of poor women from the countryside into prostitution, concubinage, and distant servitude meant a
reduction in the number of marriageable women. No longer able to
have marriages arranged for them, local men turned for sexual satisfaction to either the local "broken shoe," tolerated in each village,
or to the brothels of nearby cities. Ironically, those men and women
who might otherwise have been married did eventually meet, but it
was in the bed of a brothel rather than on the *k'ang* of a poor man's
hut.[48]

Sexual Economics and the Economics of Sexuality

The treatment of women in times of famine is a grim and gripping
story, and one that reveals men's fundamental attitudes towards
women. In normal times, females were viewed by males as merchandise to be used in their homes and then, after what the *Biographies of Famous Women* called their tenure as "guests" was over,[49]
to be disposed of. When times were good, a girl might remain with
her natal family well into adolescence. If there were sons to take
care of the parents in old age, she would then be married. When
times were bad, especially during famines, the patterns changed,
and a young female's future was often determined by the difference
between her value to the household and what she could bring in the
marketplace.

It is very difficult to put a cash value on women's work in the
domestic economy of nineteenth-century China. Women were cer-

tainly indispensable in the family economy: they performed house-
work, raised and instructed children, managed households, and
often did farm work as well. Cash from the sale of their crafts and
handiwork was an essential part of most peasant budgets. Therefore, it appears that when a female was sold a decision was made
that her "net value," the value of her domestic production over and
above the cost of her upkeep, was less than the amount for which
she could be traded. The amounts that were paid for women in the
wide variety of transactions that were made throughout their lives
give us clues to this net value.

Abject misery or greed could cause females to be sold for very
small sums. In one instance, a gambler traded his wife to pay a debt
of two dollars and fifty cents.[50] A good index of women's value,
however, was the required bride price, which served as compensation for surrendered work. The amount varied according to region,
class, and whether the female was given over as an adopted
daughter-in-law or adult bride. In the worst of times, families sold
baby girls as adopted daughters for only a few dollars. Generally,
less than ideal marriages—for example, those in which the bride was
an adopted daughter, or had been a servant, or in which the future
husband was a widower—might be contracted for three to ten *taels*
($2-7.50). Marriage of adult brides in more elite circles brought in
from several hundred to several thousand *taels* but required a more
impressive dowry as well.[51] Although for most parents, marriage was
the most respectable way of disposing of their daughters, it generally did not garner a great deal of ready cash.

A less desirable, but often more readily available, means of disposing of a daughter was selling her into domestic service. Parents
could hope that the girl would be incorporated into a kind family
who would arrange an adequate marriage for her. The risks in this
transfer were greater than in a simple marriage transaction, since a
servant would not have the shield of children to redeem her and an
employer might treat her harshly or even resell her. Sale as servant
or slave, if total control were relinquished, might net 20-300 *taels*
($15-225) for young girls, slightly more for older girls already cap-
able of heavy physical work. One western observer calculated that
the transaction would bring roughly the equivalent of $2.00 for each
year of age.[52] Sometimes the purchases were camouflaged under the
adopted daughter rubric, but the basic intention was to obtain a
domestic worker, not a family member.

Also second best but grudgingly accepted was the sale of a daughter, widow, or even wife as a concubine. Generally, a concubine acted as a servant to the principal wife and was treated by law as roughly equivalent to a household servant. She was often expected to serve the sexual appetite of an aging man and had no independent status in the household. In contrast to the primary wife, she did not receive status through her sons, who were regarded juridically as children of the husband and the principal wife.

It is difficult to find references in the late Ch'ing to families selling their daughters directly into concubinage, since many were reluctant to do so except in times of extreme duress. An early Ch'ing source states that the price for such a sale then was 100-200 *taels* ($75-150).[53] Men usually bought concubines from managers of brothels and teahouses who charged high prices as compensation for their lost income.[54]

The least socially desirable sale, yet the most profitable for the seller, was into prostitution. Prices for prostitutes varied enormously, depending on the woman's virginity, age, beauty, background, and whether she was bought directly from her relatives or through some sort of middleman. The initial purchase price was often multiplied severalfold as the victim passed from kidnapper, bandit group, or initial buyer to the procurer for a brothel or teahouse.[55] A girl sold by parents as a prostitute would bring two or three times the amount paid for a servant.[56] In the occasional references in the literature, we find prices for direct family sale to procurers that range from a few dollars to several hundred, depending on age, attractiveness, and entertainment skills. Old Lady Ning's little daughter was sold by her father to a procurer for only 3,500 cash ($3.50); a prostitute in *Travels of Lao Ts'an* was bought from her family for $24; and Old Lady Ning's son-in-law wanted to sell his older daughter as a sing-song girl for 300 *taels* ($225).[57] Sometimes, the amount was determined strictly by age. A magistrate in Szechuan bought girls of seven and eight for $8-10, young women sixteen to seventeen for $40-50, if they were single, and $20 if they were married.[58]

Prices for the cheapest sales varied widely, depending largely on the degree of parental desperation, the greediness of ruthless relatives, the local supply, and the intended use and saleability of the young woman. A set of standard prices prevailed in the large cities where a good deal of trading was done and a system of brokers had developed. Lower-class brothels paid about $30-50 for their women; middle-class establishments perhaps $50-150; and upper-class houses $150-300 for courtesans if they bought them when young, but $200-3,000 if they were older and had some training.[59]

This is not to suggest that parents were in possession of all this information or that their decisions were always clear-cut and rational. Yet, considering the options available for poorer women, a sale into servitude or even prostitution was not always an irrational choice on the part of the parents. Like much of the traditional "slavery" in Africa, Chinese adoption and sale can be seen as crude social welfare institutions.[60]

Yet, the disposal of wives and daughters highlights the fundamental difference between the way men and women were regarded in Chinese society. One student of another culture captured the essence of this difference in her title, *Women of Value, Men of Renown.*[61] Whether purchased, pawned, bought and sold as adopted daughters, future daughters-in-law and adult brides, or "sold" as prostitutes for a night's sex or entertainment, women were regarded fundamentally as disposable merchandise, as commodities. The prostitute's singularity lay in being a strictly sexual commodity.

The combination of disintegration and disequilibrium in the late Imperial and early Republican period brought many changes to the Chinese, including alterations in their values. In the twentieth century cities, as we shall see, prostitutes could more openly practice their profession, which came to be regarded as more economically and more morally viable. Yet these alterations of values could occur because prostitution was already changing in late Ch'ing times. It was actually only a short step from the familial "green bower" of the nineteenth century, filled with women whose parents may have been only dimly aware of this fate, to the dance halls and cheap brothels of the twentieth century. With the fall of Imperial China and the emergence of new elites, the distance was easily crossed. "Beautiful merchandise" was the strand that connected prostitutes in the two eras and revealed the sexual economy that underlay the fate of women in both Imperial and Republican China.

CHAPTER FOUR: TRANSFORMATIONS AND TRANSVALUATIONS 1911–1936

A brief article in a 1923 Chinese magazine[1] offers a tantalizing glimpse into the world of "female entertainers." The authorities in Shanghai had decided to streamline legal categories and classify together as prostitutes all women employed in teahouses, inns, hotels, floating flower boats, and brothels for the purposes of registration, licensing, and taxation. In response, the women who regarded themselves as the elite of the profession took to the streets. In parades and demonstrations they appealed to the general public to support customs that were centuries old. The banners they bore aloft defiantly proclaimed the traditional motto of "singing girls:" *chih mai k'ou, pu mai shen* (we sell only our voices, not our bodies). A letter they submitted to the authorities argued their case: they were artists, not prostitutes, and classifying all women entertainers together was outrageous.

This little anecdote suggests several intriguing questions: What actually were the various female entertainment professions by the twentieth century? How were "sing-song girls" different from the common prostitutes, with whom they so disliked being associated? Why were they appealing to the public for support? Also, why were city officials making these changes—out of impulses for moral reform or for social control? Was the situation in other urban areas similar to that of Shanghai or was cosmopolitan Shanghai an exception? Finally, were these women native to Shanghai, recent rural migrants new to city life, or educated "modern" women influenced by western attitudes and life-styles?

The twenty-five years from 1911 to 1936 were an era of change and flux, of continuities and discontinuities. All sectors of society were changing—peasants were becoming farmers, masters employers, merchants businessmen, and workers proletarians. After the final collapse of the traditional Chinese state and before the total disruption of the society by the Japanese invasion, the old social rules no longer applied, but new ones had yet to be formulated. By the end of the period, two alternative visions of the future, which had begun to crystallize in the early 1920s, had hardened into opposing political camps, one Nationalist, the other Communist. The issue was no longer whether China would change but instead how much, to what degree, and in which direction.

The new urban society was the arena for most of the major transformations in Chinese society. One change was the disintegration of central authority, accompanied by a shifting and often disruptive struggle for control. Another was the increasing immiseration of the rural population that caused increased migration to cities where there were few opportunities for even marginal employment. Growing pauperization of both rural and urban dwellers led parents and family members to reconsider their views about female futures. Another change was the evolution of a very different social structure, in many ways the opposite of the Confucian ideal of earlier Chinese society. A new set of urban attitudes represented an amalgam of traditional and modern, but was distinctly modern in many respects. Those familiar with the China of the early twentieth century often spoke about how it differed from the China of the nineteenth century. If we examine these changes and try to understand how they impinged on women and particularly on prostitutes, we will more fully comprehend how the western-trained Chinese sociologist, Yen Ching-yüeh, could assert in 1934 that in the twentieth century, prostitution, like China, had been utterly transformed.[2]

Sources for the twentieth century are vastly improved over those for the nineteenth. The work of foreign observers is complemented by detailed observatons of Chinese society by Chinese authors who were often students of the emerging western social sciences. Thus, rural investigations and city surveys by individual analysts are available along with studies done by religious groups and international commissions and organizations. Additional information comes from the media, which became a separate entity in the twentieth century and began to reflect new social realities and modern interests. Newspapers advertised the social amusements of the day. Photographs of courtesans were displayed, their social activities were gossiped about, and their troubles were an integral part of the police blotter and human interest sections. A good deal of fiction was originally published in newspapers, journals, and tabloids. In fact, the fiction of this period is even a more reliable source of information because of the growing emphasis on social realism.[3]

The above sources must, of course, be used with great caution, but careful scrutiny of the evidence reveals compelling patterns. Extensive material exists for the North of China, particularly the area around Peking in modern day Hopei and Honan provinces. The remainder of this study will therefore focus on that area.

Shifting Struggles for Control

The history of Peking, an administrative capital since the thirteenth century, has been shaped largely by politics, and the early twentieth century was no exception. The period from 1911 to 1936 was difficult for the people of North China. The bewildering political chronology of the period reflects the considerable instability in the area, which was often swept by warfare. There were at least eight changes in the head of state, and outright war broke out among military cliques in 1920, 1922, and 1924.[4] Peking felt the effects of this struggle for control because it was the seat of government until 1927–28, and because disruptions caused people in the surrounding towns and villages to look to Peking for refuge and relief.

The struggle of militarists (often derogatorily called "warlords") and politicians for control of the region had demonstrable effects on both the supply of and demand for prostitutes in urban centers. The devastation wrought by the armies of the warlords caused rural residents—especially males—to flee their homes. They also left to escape being drafted into military service, seeking employment in nearby cities. Without wives, and without families or funds to help them obtain brides, they turned to prostitutes in cheap brothels for sexual gratification. The soldiers themselves formed a major part of the growing demand for prostitutes. Nearly every commentator on social life in China in this period, such as the American Sidney Gamble in his 1922 social survey of Peking, noted that "the soldiers are probably the most immoral of any class of men in China."[5] They often forcibly took women from the local populations or else bought the services of destitute rural women whose husbands had left or been drafted. Short stories from the period tell of this peculiar "brothelization" of the countryside.[6]

Warlord armies and the turmoil they produced in the countryside greatly increased the number of young women available for prostitution in rural and, eventually, urban areas. Unpaid or underpaid soldiers abducted or purchased poor women and then resold them into prostitution. Officers, too, were frequently accused of taking this opportunity to augment their incomes.[7] The warlords' ever increasing need for money also resulted in a growing financial burden for many Chinese families. New taxes were imposed on many commodities, and bribes exacted by tax collectors hit small merchants and landowners especially hard. These heavy burdens became particularly onerous when they coincided with other catastrophes, such as famine and drought in the 1920s and depression in the 1930s. After 1932, the combination of global economic downturn and warlord devastation wreaked havoc on the rural economy.[8] Hardship forced parents to sell daughters and other female family members or migrate to cities where their women were often pawned to brothels, sold into fictitious marriages, or employed in positions that eventually led them into prostitution.

It is necessary, therefore, to understand the intricate calculations made by twentieth-century families who found their well-being severely threatened. What were the options as they saw them, and how were these alternatives regarded and weighted? What part, in other words, did prostitution play in the ongoing survival strategies available to China's rural and urban poor?

Sexual Economies and Demographic Strategies

Large families had always been the ideal in China, but the hard reality was that many children, especially females, could be a tremendous burden on families. Abortion and infanticide had always been used extensively to limit family size and dispose of undesired offspring. The traditional methods of abortion (drinking various mixtures and applying pressure to the fetus) and birth control (abstinence and breast feeding) were still used in the twentieth century, particularly by poor women but also by the upper classes.[9] Yet, there were signs of change. It appears that, just as fewer young women's feet were bound, fewer girl babies were drowned, smothered, and abandoned.

This change presents a contradiction: more female children were being rescued from infanticide at a time when economic conditions were worsening for some and certainly not improving for most.[10] This might be explained in part by the changing economic options for women, since in the twentieth century there were increasing employment opportunities in the handful of industrializing urban areas. But this was not enough to account for the change. Other factors clearly were at work.

Traditionally, Chinese families sought to keep sons and daughters at home until they were of marriageable age, when, after elaborate negotiations, sons would bring in brides and daughters would marry out. Yet, as we saw in the nineteenth century, this ideal often could not be realized, and other ways had to be found to dispose of daughters. *Yang nü* adoption was one of the most popular. In the twentieth century, as a League of Nations Report in 1933 argued, the "adopted daughter" institution was increasingly resorted to by parents and further distorted from its original function as a humane social welfare institution.[11] By exopting daughters, parents were able to dispose of girls early and get needed cash, even though they lost full or partial rights over their offspring. It appears, then, that females were saved from infanticide only to be disposed of before marriageable age. Poorer men lamented their inability to locate adult brides: "Wives are hard to get nowadays, and wherever they come from we are glad to welcome them," a Peking peddler told an interviewer in the early 1930s.[12] Families, aware that they could no longer afford to wait and marry off their daughters at an appropriate age, found that there existed other, more lucrative alternatives.

Women who lived in or nearby cities and towns had always been able to contribute to the family economy in other ways than by being sold. They participated in traditional home crafts and industries which produced an important part of the income of families confronted by uncertain and variable markets for agricultural goods. Urban women also contributed to small family businesses, and there must have been quite a few fathers, like the one in *Rickshaw Boy,* a famous proletarian novel of the 1930s, who secretly wished his daughter would not marry but continue to work for his business.[13] The traditional service jobs open to women in cities—peddling and household and brothel service—had low prestige and were often resorted to in lieu of begging or prostitution, since in the twentieth century as in the nineteenth, these positions were regarded with opprobrium.[14]

Increasingly in the twentieth century, a new set of alternatives, although admittedly few in number, opened in cities, undoubtedly affecting the calculations many parents either explicitly or implicitly made in developing their survival strategies. In industrial areas like the lower Yangtze delta in Central China and certain cities like Tientsin and Mukden in the North, there were increasing opportunities for women in industry. Women were employed extensively by the textile industry, in tobacco and match manufacturing, and in the initial processing of raw materials such as cotton, wool, nut and seed oils. Families in surrounding areas became increasingly aware of these new options.[15] Jobs in industry were not yet available in non-industrial cities like Peking, but even here there seems to have been more cottage work. A few other service positions were opening up for women, such as hostess jobs in restaurants.

But the most important urban outlet now used by families seeking new survival strategies was the market for pawned females. Women were pawned into positions ranging from household servant to concubine. But there is a great deal of evidence that destitute families increasingly viewed the pawning of females into brothels and teahouses as an acceptable alternative. The father of a poor city girl in *Rickshaw Boy* urged her to mortgage herself to a brothel long before she resignedly did so.[16] Prostitution, after all, was comparatively lucrative and positions were readily available. Pawning, which came to be seen as a fortuitous compromise, was certainly more advantageous to families than outright sale, which denied them any of the woman's future income. If a daughter was pawned as a prostitute, some of her income could return to the family. The daughter-prostitute was in the process of becoming a family wage earner.[17]

There is also evidence that this reordering of economic priorities due to increasing economic insecurity forced a change in values. The 1933 League of Nations Report, reinforced by fictional accounts,[18] suggests that many prostitutes regarded participation in their profession as part of their filial duty to care for family members as best they could. Parents increasingly appealed to this distorted sense of *li* to make more palatable what had previously been shameful and degrading. Essentially, economic decisions had been camouflaged as moral imperatives.

A Shifting Social Structure

Radical changes in the concept of *li* were possible because a very different China was evolving during the years 1911 to 1936. The arbiters and notions of *li* were not the same in the 1930s as they had been in 1910 on the eve of the fall of the last dynasty. As China "entered the modern age," its traditional social structure was greatly altered. A significant change was the rise of a new elite which actually had been evolving since the late Ch'ing dynasty. Like the old mandarins, members of the new elite defined standards of propriety, including those for women in general and prostitutes in particular.

In a flawed but perceptive analysis of the structural changes occurring in Republican China, Martin C. Yang offers a useful typology of the elite.[19] It was composed of new-style militarists, the new intelligentsia, a reoriented upper and lower gentry, and new businessmen. The new militarists were composed of three types: those, like the northerner Yuan Shih-k'ai, were formally educated in the traditional manner and wanted to increase their power according to the traditional bounds of rule. Others, like the northern warlord Chang Tso-lin, had bandit connections or were from "local bully" backgrounds, and wanted only to increase their power at the expense of the people. The third type, like another northerner Feng Yü-hsiang, also from peasant origins but through contact with the West able to blend notions of progressive reform with traditional beliefs, wanted to increase their rule in the interests of, and representing the will of, the people.[20]

The new intelligentsia were products of new economic, social, and political conditions and often spanned both upper and middle classes. Increasingly at the forefront of political debate, they had a "modern" mentality which considered business, professional, and other white collar occupations to be as desirable as scholarly or official positions and which emphasized change and modernity over tradition and conservatism. By 1927–28, they were polarized politically between the Nationalists and Communists.[21]

The gentry were those members of the elite whose wealth was mostly invested in land. They usually had important roles as landlords and had been bulwarks of Confucian social traditions. Yet, they had a somewhat ambiguous allegiance both to the state and to their local communities. Individual members of this gentry group differed markedly in their reorientation during this period. Though most had received a traditional upbringing, and many held firmly to traditional social values and moral beliefs, some were able with varying degrees of skill and consistency to graft western education and views onto a Confucian base.[22] Others either rejected western notions and adhered strictly to traditional Confucian ideas or else embraced new ideas, such as Marxism, Socialism, or democracy. Yet in spite of the persistence of a few adherents to tradition, nearly every member of this elite believed that China needed some sort of change and development, and all agreed that local communities and regions should have more voice in government.[23]

The fourth category contained the new businessmen, including merchants, financiers, and industrialists. Many were traditional gentry who had been able to assimilate and synthesize a new, quasi-modern ethos based on traditional Confucian values and learning. Some were the products of a westernized eduction and training in modern business techniques, rather than men who had acquired their business acumen by apprenticeship and personal experience in the old style. Yet their prestige in society was not solely due to their new-style education and training, but also to a belief that their own strength and prosperity could lead to China's renewed strength and vigor. They began to be valued for their wealth and power rather than for the old, idealized standards of moral integrity and virtue. Their new-found acceptance and their link with a strong China allowed businessmen to take on a public leadership role and make their displays of wealth and prestige more visible. The important role played by the new Chambers of Commerce in local governments and the assumption of official posts by many businessmen are but two examples of this new public toleration and respect.[24]

Changes in the male elite profoundly affected women, especially prostitutes and female entertainers. The persistence of traditional "long gown" Confucian gentlemen and, even among the more progressive, of habits belonging to them, insured the continued demand for traditional wives, concubines, and entertainers. Yet the demand for old-style women was diminishing. Instead, among new-style militarists, the twentieth-century intelligentsia and the more modern, reoriented gentry, the predominant desire was for modern, educated women, as wives, sex partners, and entertainers. It was not uncommon for gentry even in the interior to desire a modern woman as primary or secondary wife.[25] When elites sought out women for entertainment, sexual, and social purposes, they increasingly preferred those women who at least had a veneer of modernity, even if only in dress and personal style. Moreover, with the embrace of a western-defined modernity came a shift in values and attitudes that presaged a new view of the relations between the sexes. A new culture was emerging in China, and with it new stan-

dards of propriety were developing. The new-style elites were slowly
rewriting the old rules of *li,* presenting in the process confusing
social messages to both urban and rural Chinese.

Transvaluations: The Evolution of a New Sexual Ethic

One of the more elusive concepts imported from the West during
this period was "modernity," the notion of a world in constant flux
tied to a linear idea of progress. But many of the fads and fashions
of an expanding consumer economy in the West were oddly out of
place in a centuries-old cultural milieu where the transmission of
tradition had been more highly prized than continual innovation.
Yet western notions were seized upon by an iconoclast minority.
Among the youth, to be continually changing and *"mo-teng"* (modern) became a positive attribute;[26] the worst that could be said was
that one was conservative or lagging behind (*lo-wu fen-tzu*).[27] The
desire for the modern had a great impact upon entertainment and
the related professions. What better badge of modernity than to be
a spectator of western, and by extension, modern types of entertainment? This attitude led to the introduction of new-style Chinese
drama, such as the plays of Ts'ao Yü, as well as popular dramatic
works by Ibsen, Chekhov, and O'Neill, and fiction by Dostoevsky,
Tolstoy, Balzac, and Thackeray. Modern, western-style theaters
were very popular in Peking.[28] Olga Lang, an American sociologist,
discovered that in the most western-influenced cities, a large proportion of the population read, or had read to them, modern magazines which contained much of the new fiction.[29] The growth of
popular fiction in this era attests to its attraction, although the content itself often expressed a deep ambivalence toward the modern
age.[30]

Upper-class prostitutes (or prostitute–"entertainers") in cities
were expected not just to mirror but to be on the cutting edge of
this change. No longer were they to represent the unchanging, in-
imitable ebb and flow of eternal tradition, as does the modern Japanese geisha. Instead, female entertainers were expected to titillate
with their modernity. Their flaunting of daring western dress, hair-
style, makeup, cigarettes, and liquor was intended to attract male
customers. Perhaps variety is part of the nature of sexual attraction,
but in the twentieth century it required being modern and acquiring
the progresively new, like the woman in Lao She's short story "The

Vision," with her cigarettes and high heels, or the concubine-former prostitute in a family for which the protagonist in *Rickshaw Boy* worked, who wore tight fitting dresses and heavy perfume.[31]

A second transformation in traditional attitudes was the openness with which matters relating to family, love, and sex were discussed. The new media, including journals, magazines, and newspapers called the "mosquito" press (because of their gossipy, fly-by-night character), played an important role in this new public discourse. In traditional Chinese culture, as we have seen, discussions of sex and sexual matters were usually understated or veiled and relegated to the private domain. The coming of the West and the experimentation with a western-oriented culture ended this bifurcation between public and private. Instead, in the pages of women's magazines and journals and in the gossip and letter columns of newspapers, people poured forth their concerns, worries, and frustrations. The introduction of the alien notion that attraction and romantic love could be the basis of marriage made people uncertain and, for the first time, rather open. Yet as the testimonies show, the openness itself was produced by anxiety. The stories and tales which filled the pages of journals and magazines demonstrate an ambivalence toward a western modernity, most often among women, who appear experimental yet anxious, seeking the new, but profoundly dissatisfied.[32] The stark truth was that this new cultural style was alien and uncomfortable—and somehow not really Chinese.

These changes can be ascribed only in part to a deliberate process of cultural imperialism.[33] Westernization was the result of several interacting factors and accompanied the loss of power and legitimacy by the old scholarly elite after China's defeats by western powers and Japan and the elimination of the examination system. By the 1920s and 30s their culture and world view appeared insufficient and unacceptable to many Chinese, and their traditional solutions seemed irrelevant and inappropriate for the problems of the twentieth century. The new elites turned to western learning and thought to remedy China's difficulties and inability to deal adequately with the West and a westernizing Japan. As a logical consequence western cultural forms were also adopted, both to legitimate and to add a fashionable foreign touch to new institutions and patterns of thinking.

Moreover, western notions and cultural forms appealed to members of the new elite, who had either assimilated and then rejected a

Confucian socialization or, by the 1930s, were products of the new learning. To all these groups a veneer of western life and style acted as a badge of identification, gave them status in the eyes of other elites, and provided a justification for their rejection of traditional values. The transitional period in contemporary Chinese history witnessed the development of a new language of status, a combination of the traditional and the modern. The new elite now demanded a woman who sported a more shapely Chinese tunic and pants, high heels and makeup, and who was simultaneously subservient yet smart, docile yet daring.

Peking: A New Urban Setting

Between 1900 and 1935, Chinese cities were the arena in which these transformations converged. The cities themselves were physically transformed. "Wide streets take the place of narrow, ill-smelling alleys," wrote an American in the 1930s. "All mechanical gadgets of our civilization have been taken over and put to work . . . the Chinese are able successfully to function as a modern corporate society."[34] It was clear, even to the naive observer, that cities like Peking had been revitalized and reshaped since the deterioration of many of their functions and the disintegration of their unifying ethos during the last dynasty.

Even before the establishment of treaty ports in the early nineteenth century, approximately 10 to 12 percent of the Chinese population had lived in cities. City dwellers were not just those connected with the administrative functions of many urban centers; approximately one-half had engaged in commerce.[35] Traditionally, much of the population was not of local origin. The local administrator and many of the merchants and small traders were men sent from distant places to pursue a profession or trade and enrich the family coffers. The twentieth century saw a continuation of this pattern. Gentry families still sent sons to schools or training institutes in urban areas. When their education was over, the young men either returned to the family estate or remained in official, military, or commercial positions in the cities.

In the twentieth century, however, the population of Chinese cities changed drastically, due in large part to increased migration by those we can call the "new sojourners"—poor men from rural towns and villages who migrated in search of work and to escape destitution or the draft. The "new sojourner" usually did not perceive himself as an urbanite solidly rooted in the city; in fact, he was expected to remit a large proportion of his income back to family and kin in his native place. In the 1940s, the anthropologist Fei Hsiao-t'ung commented on the phenomenon of urban transients and likened the possibility of returning home to a type of unemployment insurance. Even when successful, these men hoped eventually to return and spend the remainder of their days in their places of origin. "The mind is here but not the heart," one man told Dr. Fei.[36] In reality, few returned, and as Sidney Gamble discovered in Peking, they were all forced to adjust to being new urbanites, as deracinated and dislocated as the migrant poor of Rio, Bombay, or Kinshasa.[37]

From 1911 to 1928, Peking was the capital of a republic, rather than the center of an imperial dynasty. Its Manchu population was no longer government supported, and its affairs of state were in chaos. In the ten-year period following Yuan Shih-k'ai's 1916 attempt at imperial restoration, Peking, meaning "northern capital," held that distinction in name only. Its hold on the rest of the country was tenuous, and the struggle for control between two military cliques was indecisive. After the nominal consolidation of power by Chiang K'ai-shek's Northern Expedition in 1927–28, the national capital was moved to Nanking, and Peking (changed in 1931 to Peiping, "northern peace") was reduced to a regional capital of the Hopei-Chahar government. This last change meant the desertion of Peiping for the new national capital by the political elite and their entourage. It also meant that those who remained frequently suffered both a loss of identity and position.

Although no longer the national capital after 1927–28, Peking still contained a sizeable foreign settlement, with foreigners living either in the so-called Legation Quarter or in areas like the Old City. Peking retained a decidedly international flavor and was influenced by the West much more than provincial capitals in the interior, but the absolute number of foreigners was relatively small, perhaps 5 to 8 percent of a total population of 811,556 in 1917.[38] Clearly, the changes visible in urban centers like Peking were due not only to the presence of a foreign population but to a Chinese elite increasingly versed in things western.

The urban middle and upper classes were far more influenced by the West than either the urban lower classes or the rural gentry and peasantry. Not only had their education and professions changed considerably, but their life-style also had been affected by changes in marriage patterns, childrearing, fashion, decorating, diet, and household conveniences.[39] External changes were matched by changes in attitude, many of which were western in origin. A new sense of urban responsibility was slowly developing. In the past, a combination of private and public associations had taken joint responsibility for the public philanthropy that existed, but it was neither enough nor sufficiently wide-ranging to solve all the new urban problems. A new vision for the cities was articulated by urban middle- and upper-class members of new, western-inspired associations like the Chambers of Commerce and the Young Men's Christian Association and members of revitalized guild and voluntary associations who had the wealth and skills to put that vision into practice. They promoted recreation for young men and women and struggled for such reforms as an all-city lighting and water supply, renovated public thoroughfares, and garbage removal. They were also involved in literacy and public health campaigns, labor arbitration, and the regulation of child labor. Yet as the decades progressed, Peking's elite became increasingly westernized, sophisticated—and more sharply and deliberately differentiated from the rest of Chinese society. More and more, reforms benefited only the privileged few.[40] Of course, this stratification was not new; what had changed was that suits and slit dresses had replaced the silken gowns and tunics of the past as the visible symbols of superior status.[41]

Peking had changed in other ways and for other inhabitants as well. By the mid-1930s, the population of what had become Peiping was nearly a million, an increase of one-quarter million in fifteen years.[42] The growing urban population was a poorer one as well. Sidney Gamble's survey of the late teens claimed that 11 percent of the population was poor. But a Peking police survey of 1926 that included beggars who lived outside the city walls showed 17 percent of the total population as destitute, 9.2 percent as poor, and 47.2 percent as lower-middle class. By contrast, only 22 percent was comfortable, and 4 percent well-to-do.[43] Observers in the 1920s and '30s agreed that economic conditions for many of the city's inhabitants were steadily worsening. This was due only in part to changing economic conditions and the status of the city itself; it also reflected the migration to the city of dislocated and destitute people. The extent of migration becomes clear if one analyzes the city population by age, sex, and income. In 1917, 63.5 percent of the total population was male; in other words, there were 174 males to every 100 females. This figure varied according to district; in the business and industrial parts of the city, as much as 72 percent of the population was male; in residential areas, the male population varied between 49.2 percent and 66.5 percent.[44]

The age structure of the male population is even more striking. Compared to American cities of similar size, Peking had an unusually high proportion of males aged twenty-five to fifty and relatively few under fifteen years of age. Males were 59 percent of those aged one to five but rose to 69 percent of those twenty-six to thirty. The proportion of males then gradually declined to 54 percent among those aged eighty or over.[45]

Their urban occupations actually reflected a wide variety of backgrounds and motivations for migration. The unskilled often became rickshaw pullers (there were fifty to sixty thousand in the 1920s) or if they were at least barely literate, policeman (there were perhaps ten thousand in the 1920s).[46] Others were semi-skilled workers, traders and small merchants, and a few migrants took highly skilled jobs or became large-scale enterpreneurs and officials. In addition, a sizeable number of the males in the city were students, since 14 of the 107 Chinese universities, colleges and technical schools were located in Peking.[47] This lent the city the air of an intellectual capital and added to the population of males a segment that was only temporarily poor.

The implications of this profile for women in general, and prostitutes in particular, were striking. Although most men in the city were married (only 9 percent of those over twenty-five and 7 percent of those over thirty were single) most of the younger males were migrants who had left their wives behind.[48] These men frequently sought out females. If they had money, they could go to the well-advertised restaurants and teahouses that provided gambling, feasting, and other amusements, the cinemas and theaters that presented western-inspired drama, and western-style dance halls, hotels, and nightclubs. Popular actresses were avidly followed from production to production. Well-known courtesans, primarily women from first- and second-class houses, often performed in theaters, which increased their popularity and gave them opportunities for assignations with appreciative members of the audience. Women similar to high-priced western call girls rented hotel rooms.[49] In order to compete and attract the best customers, these women had to be *au courant* and among the first to sport the most provocative western styles. Since these accoutrements were expensive, only upper-class prostitutes or women kept by wealthy men could afford them.

Urban males who had neither money nor leisure either sought out the cheap women available on the street or visited the "white-houses." Lower-class women and houses showed little influence from the West—a bit of garish makeup, a cheap picture tacked to the wall or a calendar advertising a tobacco company.[50] All the rest—the outrageous behavior, the lewd songs and catchwords—were traditionally Chinese.

The growing demand for both cheap, traditional prostitutes and expensive, "modern" women caused a change in the distribution of brothels and teahouses in Peking. By 1930, there were half as many first and second-level establishments as in 1919, one-quarter more third-level houses, and twice as many fourth-level houses.[51] Not all houses were licensed, but the majority of those unlicensed were probably lower than first class since the latter were too visible and too intimately linked with elite and official circles to go unregistered. It appears that there was a levelling of the institution, with more establishments provided for the increasing numbers of poor males. But this was only part of the story. At the same time that there was an increase in the number of lower-class prostitutes, the courtesan was transformed into a western-style entertainer. This change was not caught in the official statistics, but was much mourned, even by the western-educated elite.

Brothels, moreover, may not have been mere victims of circumstances, springing up to meet the demands of the "new sojourner." The Board of Police set the number of brothels in each category and thus was responsible for permitting more brothels to be available to the poor. It is quite possible that this reflected a new urban policy of placation. Instead of "bread and circuses," the Chinese seem to have chosen "brothels and congee" for controlling new urban marginals. Perhaps this accounts in part for the ease with which unlicensed prostitutes were able to bribe the local police into granting them immunity from prosecution. The police may have been instructed to suppress only establishments that overtly offended public sensibilities, as defined by Chinese and foreign officials, entrepreneurs, and diplomats. "Orderly" brothels were encouraged since they supplied urgently needed urban revenue while satisfying the disoriented—and potentially disaffected and dangerous—urban poor.

In sum, Peking, like other cities, experienced the emergence of a new urbanism in the twentieth century. It was shaped by a new elite differentiated from the masses of the population by a western-defined modernity. At the same time, Peking hosted a still traditional poor who had few economic and moral options. Male demands for rest and recreation were more sharply delineated: they either sought new-style women or the more traditional common prostitutes. The new-style women conferred a sense of modernity, while the hard pressed harlot helped to defuse the dissatisfaction of new urban marginals. In the process, the Shanghai sing-song girls completed that long journey that separated their twentieth-century street demonstrations from the secluded performances of female entertainers of distant dynasties.

CHAPTER FIVE: A PICTURE OF TWENTIETH-CENTURY PROSTITUTION

Beyond the Eight Great Lanes

Twentieth-century China inherited the traditional types of brothels that had developed over the centuries. There were still registered first- and second-class establishments resembling restaurants, and, as mentioned earlier, there was an apparent increase in the number of third-class houses, which were more clearly brothels. Fourth- and fifth-class houses proliferated during this period. In addition, there seems to have been a large number of clandestine prostitutes who lived either in unregistered, organized brothels or who operated out of private homes and hotel rooms. During the early decades of the twentieth century, the influx of poor women into cities and the emergence of the independent "modern" woman appear to have accounted for an increase in the latter category.

There had been repeated attempts in Chinese history to limit brothels to a special quarter of the city. Novels and painting of various periods portray colorful and lively entertainment districts. In Peking the district was traditionally near Willow Lane (*Liu li hsiang*), but after the Boxer Rebellion of 1898-1900 and the subsequent reorganization of the city it was moved to an area just outside the southwest gate, known as the "Eight Big Lanes" (*Pa ta hu-t'ung*). Soon licensed brothels could be found in other areas as well: in the South City area called "Big Luxurious Neighborhood" (*Ta sen li*) and outside the city in the "Yellow Crane Tower" district (*Huang he lou*).[1] In 1918, the Board of Police erected modern buildings in the east section of the Old City to house the brothels, but the proprietors refused to move, preferring their familiar traditional and semi-modern buildings.[2] Unlicensed brothels and streetwalkers were located all over the city, but two concentrations of them—one containing many foreign women (Japanese, Russians, and other Europeans) and another containing only Manchu women—were near the foreign legations in the southeast and eastern parts of the Old City.[3]

MAP 1. Distribution of Four Levels of Brothels in Peiping, adapted by Anita O'Brien from map in Mai Ch'ien-tseng, "Pei p'ing ch'ang chi tiao ch'a" (Survey of Prostitution in Peiping), *She hui hsueh chieh* 5 (1931).

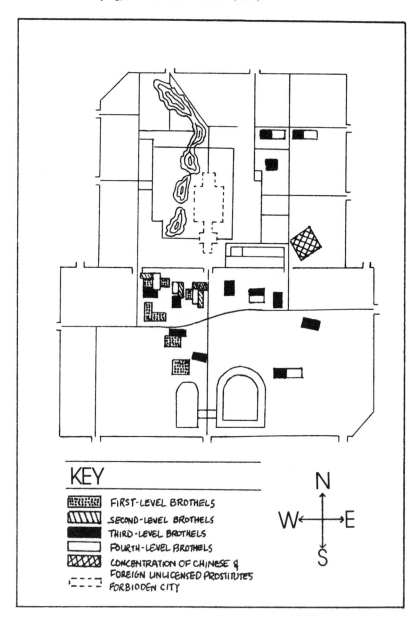

KEY

FIRST-LEVEL BROTHELS

SECOND-LEVEL BROTHELS

THIRD-LEVEL BROTHELS

FOURTH-LEVEL BROTHELS

CONCENTRATION OF CHINESE & FOREIGN UNLICENSED PROSTITUTES

FORBIDDEN CITY

Independent, unlicensed prostitutes seem to have run the gamut from the educated and modern to the appallingly poor and deprived. Chen Pai-lu, the main character in the play "Sunrise" by Ts'ao Yü, is strikingly similar to a western high-class call girl. Like Zola's Nana, she was kept by several admirers in a grand hotel, had freedom to select her favorites and, although the author is somewhat ambiguous on this point, was probably sexually involved with them in exchange for her upkeep.[4] The main character of Lao She's short story "Crescent Moon" was a primary school graduate without family support who discovered that her education did not increase her employment opportunities. Her only options were to work at poorly paid, degrading jobs, such as restaurant hostess, or become an independent streetwalker like her mother and look for a man to support her.[5] She chose to rent cheap rooms where she entertained regular customers for a living which, the author suggests, was adequate to meet her needs.[6]

The real women these fictional characters represent can be seen as victims of an uneven modernization. Young women with some education found few options open to them. Their only respectable choices were to agree to a traditional marriage or try to obtain one of the few clerical or primary school teaching positions that were available. But these jobs could barely support even one person, and many women still had familial obligations. Thus it appears that some western-educated, or merely western-influenced, "modern" women became call girls as a means of earning a living, while others were also attracted by the independent, modern life-style.

The other type of independent prostitute, the streetwalker, was the poorest of poor women, who had to entice customers without the aid of a formal establishment. They were like the poor young woman in *Rickshaw Boy* who was encouraged by her father to become a prostitute and add to the family's meager income. She hesitated joining a brothel because she would have been forced to sell herself entirely to the establishment. Instead, she became an independent streetwalker and solved the problem of where to conduct her business by renting a friend's bedroom during the day.[7]

It is impossible to tell the true extent of unlicensed prostitution, whether by high-class call girls or poor streetwalkers. The authorities considered any apartment or house that contained even one prostitute to be an unlicensed brothel which must be registered and brought under the control of the police. According to foreign accounts, independent prostitutes were most prevalent in the bigger cities like Peking, yet their presence was rarely felt.[8] In a society that assumed everyone belonged to a unit, preferably a stable, cohesive kinship group, prostitutes and customers preferred the organized brothel. The life of an independent prostitute may have been free of madams and proprietors, but it was too insecure for most women. It lacked protection against loneliness, patrons, and the police.

Falling into the Water

In common parlance, there were three kinds of prostitutes in brothels—free, sold, and pawned. "Pawned" prostitutes (*ya chang*), who reflected the confluence of economic forces and social values discussed earlier, formed the majority, at least by the early 1930s.[9] In most instances, a pawned prostitute was an impoverished young woman who had been mortgaged to a brothel by parents or other relatives. She was, quite literally, an item of collateral. Her relatives received a flat sum as a loan, and during her career a portion of her income would accrue to her family. Theoretically, the prostitute could be released when her relatives had paid back the original loan plus the standard 30 percent interest. Women in these circumstances were often referred to as "debt" prostitutes.[10]

The poor, traditional women who submitted to these arrangements had no recourse to outside defenders, no other way to earn a living, absolutely no other options. In a society like China's, running away was difficult; rural communities had few unattached people, and runaways could be easily discovered. There was no accessible underworld in urban areas in which young women could be safely submerged and no one on whom they could rely for protection and care. Moreover, debt prostitutes were almost always placed in brothels by relatives who knew the consequences of the pawn and who often kept up contact, if only for revenue. A woman's obligation to be filial and supply her family's needs was often so strong that the last thing she would have considered was refusing them, even if she herself opposed the decision and suffered its consequences.[11] Increasingly in the twentieth century, one reads of parents and relatives placing females in brothels with the women's full awareness and compliance, if not always agreement.[12] What is lacking is a sense of their own reactions to being used as family collateral in the service of men's sexual needs.

"Sold" prostitutes seem to have been the second most common inmates of brothels. As in the nineteenth century, the majority had not been sold into prostitution initially. Slavery had been forbidden by law in 1906, and even though sanctions against it were not enforced until the mid-1930s, there was less overt slavery in the early twentieth century. Instead the "adopted daughter" rubric was conveniently used to disguise the outright sale of women. Young girls frequently passed through entrepreneurial intermediaries who included military personnel, officials, and businessmen with wide national contacts.[13]

After 1911, fewer establishments were willing to purchase very young girls and then raise and train them in entertainment and sexual skills. They preferred the less time-consuming and cheaper practice of procuring older girls and young women from their parents. Females from newly impoverished families were considered to be the best candidates, since they had better manners and breeding than those from families long enmeshed in poverty.[14] But newly poor families were generally reluctant to send female members directly to brothels and teahouses. Proprietors therefore had to rely on their procurers either to trick or kidnap young women. The literature is replete with a whole repertoire of dirty tricks employed by procurers: a widow was fooled by a woman posing as a hairdresser; a woman was given a promise of distant work by a neighbor who was actually a brothel operator; a naive lass fresh from the country was deceived by a friendly older woman in her new neighborhood; an adopted daughter-in-law was told by a neighbor that he would take her back to her parents, but he sold her instead to a brothel.[15]

Frequently the families were also deceived and females were taken away under the pretext of employment, marriage, or adoption. One famine report mentions that clever procurers were deceiving parents with false marriage papers.[16] In *Rickshaw Boy* a poor young woman returned home after being deserted by a soldier to whom she had been married for over a year. She discovered that he had devised a foolproof scheme for avoiding venereal disease while getting domestic service and regular sex wherever he was quartered. He simply paid one to two hundred dollars to "marry" a pretty, poor, young virgin in each city and then abandoned her when his unit was called up.[17] Most schemes were not so ingenious; often they simply required carrying off unattended females.[18] Kidnapping was much riskier than purchase, but it certainly was far cheaper than paying fifty to two hundred dollars for a marriage.

It appears that the combination of economic squeeze and changing values in the cities and surrounding countryside produced another source of women for purchase—"fallen women," women who had run off from their families and communities with men. In some cases, the men had been genuine lovers, in others they had falsely promised innocent country women a better life. Some of the men quickly wearied of their women and brought them to procurers; others found making a living in a hostile city too difficult and abandoned or sold their lovers; still others merely loved and left, discarding unskilled, dislocated women who had no other recourse than begging or prostitution. One after another of the Peking prostitutes interviewed by Yen Ching-yüeh recounted this tale of love, hope, and abandonment.[19] The price of modernization—and the struggle to find a modern lifestyle—was high for everyone in Chinese society, but it seemed to exact a particularly high cost from such women.

Direct purchase and deceit were methods by which brothels and teahouses procured women from within the city or from the immediate surrounding area, but they never produced enough inexpensive women to fill the brothels. Another important source was the thriving market in females from areas struck by natural disasters or political dislocation. The 1920s were not good years, especially in the North. A study of Hopei and Shantung[20] describes those years as filled with natural calamities, warfare, tax increases, and price fluctuations. During the devastations of 1920–21,[21] missionaries and others established "famine" schools, industrial training schools, and refuges for females to prevent their being sold on the open market. There was even a limited purchase policy by the Peking United International Famine Relief Committee which bought women on the market to remove them from the hands of middlemen and entrepreneurs.[22]

No aggregate statistics are available on these sales, but several significant studies were conducted. Two were published by the Peking United International Famine Relief Committee, one covering 112 sales in 33 villages, and the other 188 cases in 68 villages.[23] These were not the only sales conducted in these areas, merely those brought to the attention of relief workers, but they provide interesting data. Roughly one-half of the girls in both studies were under ten years of age and one-third were aged ten to twenty. Almost all were sold outside their home districts; one-half in one study going to other provinces where they had little chance to return home, even though repatriation orders were frequently issued after famines. The reports cite prices from $3 to $150, but the range is deceptive since the average price may have been closer to $10. Accounts in newspapers and journals support this conclusion: a girl was bought from a landlord who agreed to give her poor mother seven ounces of gold to pay for her father's coffin; a female child was bought for $6 from a starving family; a seventeen-year old daughter was sold for $17; a starving man was forced to kill his daughter when no one would buy her for $3.[24]

As in the nineteenth century, the girls and women were usually sold by parents to middlemen who resold them for a higher price at some distant place. The woman bought for seven ounces of gold was resold for ten ounces. The return on the investment could range from thirty to over one thousand percent.[25] As a result, perhaps even more frequently than before, young girls were first bought as "adopted daughters" or adopted daughters-in-law and worked until they were old enough to be resold as prostitutes, at great financial gain for the adopting families. A 1933 report by the League of Nations charged that many people were deliberately investing in women to be used as slaves, while calling them adopted, and later selling or pawning them to brothels. The report called this the largest source of women for prostitution.[26] In the nineteenth century the British had found this system virtually impossible to penetrate, and twentieth-century reformers were scarcely more successful. Their efforts were limited to providing hostels for the few women able to free themselves and leave the brothels.

The third kind of prostitute, the woman who entered a brothel of her own volition, as a free woman, was rare. The interviews conducted by Yen Ching-yüeh indicate that these women seem to have been motivated by economic hardship or maltreatment: one prostitute with whom he talked was poor and had eight people to support. Selling herself as a slave or maidservant would only have produced enough income for herself; prostitution was the only way to obtain the income she needed. "Please tell me how I can solve my problems other than by being a prostitute!" she pleaded. Others ran away to avoid beatings by husbands or mothers-in-law, only to discover they had no way to support themselves except by prostitution.[27]

In summary, the three types of prostitutes—pawned, purchased, and free—represented three paths to recruitment into prostitution and often different degrees of a woman's involvement in the decision that led her there. Pawned and free women were frequently entered in brothels with full awareness of their destination. Purchased women, on the other hand, were generally less involved in the decision and also less aware of the consequences.

A final point concerns the relative frequency of these three paths and any changes in the institution they might reflect. In the 1930s the President of the Peiping Court of Justice and the Tientsin Reform Society alleged that fewer women than before were being sold to brothels by middlemen. Increasingly, they asserted, women were either pledged (pawned) by relatives or were "volunteers."[28] Most of the prostitutes interviewed by Yen Ching-yüeh corroborated this allegation. Whether rural or urban by birth, they were overwhelmingly poor city dwellers who had been pawned or sold to brothels by relatives and lovers or forced by poverty to enter these establishments.[29] This signifies a shift in both circumstances and attitudes. In urban society when kin and community could no longer support all women, relatives and women themselves were forced to participate directly in the decision to place women in brothels. The twentieth-century prostitute was generally a poor, defenseless urban woman who not only "fell in the water" but was lost in the contradictions of the emerging new society as well.

The Life

In the twentieth century as in the nineteenth, many western observers insisted that prostitution in China was less onerous than in the raucous red light districts of the West. In China, they claimed, prostitutes were incorporated into "families," who supplied their daily needs. Unlike their western sisters, they were not exposed to sadistic pimps or dangerous johns, inclement weather, and corrupt police. But how did Chinese prostitutes themselves view their profession? Was it, moreover, better than the other alternatives available to them?

The answers to these questions vary depending on the circumstances under which a woman entered the profession and the class of establishment in which she practiced. One ex-prostitute interviewed in the 1940s believed that her life as a first-class girl was infinitely preferable to being the wife of a poor and unattractive village bumpkin. Another believed her first-class days were idyllic but her fourth-class days were a living hell.[30] But even the upper-level houses left their mark on women. Gamble, noting that women in the upper-class houses were generally sixteen to eighteen years old, observed that their faces were marked by nervous strain and tension.[31] For some, it was a race against death. "I could almost see myself dying," narrated the main character in "Cresent Moon." "With every dollar I took in, I seemed to come closer to death. Money is supposed to preserve life, but the way I earned it, it had the opposite effect. I could see myself dying; I waited for death."[32]

Vague threats of resale or ejection were not the only dangers inherent in a profession which was based solely on beauty and youth. As in the past, prostitution carried with it its own special set of occupational hazards, some physical, and others emotional. Madams and owners were not known for their kindness. They used strict rules and sharp tongues, and seem to have regularly resorted to beatings and withholding food to punish the unsubmissive or merely to keep inmates docile. A prostitute in "A Summer Night's Dream," who considered herself better off than most, could not distinguish between the marks on her legs left by mosquito bites and the welts from her "mama's" whippings.[33]

Two other physical hazards particularly associated with prostitution were, of course, pregnancy, which usually was terminated, and venereal disease, which ordinarily was not. Modern methods of contraception were still relatively unknown at this time in China.[34] Although many prostitutes eventually became sterile, in their early years they frequently became pregnant and had to abort. Detailed medical reports from the 1920s and 1930s describe the combinations of special medicines which were ingested or placed on tampons, the "violent manipulations of the uterus from the outside," and the special devices introduced into the womb, including a procedure known as "ecbolic acupuncture," placing a needle into the uterus and thus dispelling the fetus. Most of these procedures could lead to infection, illness, or even death. Women not able to locate skilled practitioners either treated themselves, like the woman who used her own knitting needle for acupuncture, or the one who inserted a chopstick in her womb, or were forced into the hands of the un-trained and unclean.[35]

Venereal disease was even more difficult to avoid. In the twenti-

eth century some western doctors estimated that 50 to 100 percent
of all prostitutes were infected. One study in Shantung in 1917
discovered that all the prostitutes who came to a dermatological
clinic were syphilitic.[36] Other studies attested to the prevalence of
venereal disease among the general population, especially among
men who were mobile and not living at home.[37] Only two Manchu-
rian cities required medical examinations for prostitutes and there
were no regular provisions for medical treatment for men or
women. Instead, people seemed to rely on thorough washing and
the "wonder" drug "606", which was widely advertised and gave a
false sense of security.[38]

A final hazard for prostitutes was the less easily measured psychological cost of "selling the skin and smile." Reference has already been made to the tension and strain exhibited by women in
the upper-level houses, and short stories often describe women as
having a tremendous toughness and coldness after being in the life.[39]
Other accounts stress the psychological damage done to women
ripped from their families and placed in generally inhospitable envi-
ronments.[40] We can only speculate how many women who had been
traded for money felt betrayed, defenseless, and despairing. Occasionally they tried flight, or the other escape that was so common
for women throughout Chinese history, suicide. In "Sunrise," a
young girl known only as "the Shrimp" finally killed herself after
being placed in a third-class brothel. The popular press frequently
recounted stories of women who committed suicide after being sold
into prostitution.[41]

However, there seems to have been a decrease in suicides in the
twentieth century, perhaps due to the numbers of women who were
pawned rather than sold outright. Pawning added an extra-filial di-
mension to prostitution. Pawned women had an obligation to carry
through their part of the arrangement and serve the family well, no
matter how onerous the task. The traditional slogan, "resentment in
their hearts and a smile on their lips," still applied to prostitutes in
the early twentieth century, but now that anger may have been
directed at relatives as much as customers.

Can we prove that most prostitutes had no choice but to submit,
starve, or commit suicide? Clearly, prostitution was not a benevo-
lent institution, and its familial face merely disguised what was a
ruthless business venture. But how did it compare with the other
options these women faced in the 1920s and 1930s? Again, the

answer seems to vary. At the two extremes of the profession, prostitution was clearly preferable. Those women who had the relative good fortune of joining upper-class houses and being considered the demi-mondaines of China were for a brief period earning more and living better than otherwise would have been possible. At the other extreme, those women who were sold as an alternative to starving with their families were at least alive. For them, prostitution was a harsh but real safety net. However, between the two poles, a judgment about the relative lives of prostitutes and poor women is very difficult to make. Poor women often led miserable lives, were ill-clothed, ill-housed, ill-fed, and overworked.[42] It is not clear that the life span of prostitutes was any shorter than that of their married sisters, many of whom died in childbirth. Twentieth-century fiction may have stressed marriage for love, but parent-arranged marriages were still the norm and both harsh mothers-in-law and overbearing husbands were quite common. By contrast, the life of a prostitute may have appeared preferable to many.

In sum, by the 1920s and 30s, although the institution had not greatly changed its external appearance and procedures, different women made their living by prostitution. Fewer seem to have entered as the result of dragnets through the famine-stricken countryside; more were poor urban or rural women who had migrated to cities or been brought there by relatives, lovers, or neighbors. The stone flower replaced the country blossom in the brothels of Peking, and in the regulations of the state, the imperatives of reform vied with the need for revenue.

CHAPTER SIX: PROSTITUTION AND PROFIT:
The Contradictions of Revenue and Reform

Reform and Women's Estate

The disintegration of the traditional Chinese order, coupled with the threat to it from outside, had far-reaching consequences. The years 1890–1910 witnessed China's traumatic defeat by Japan, the convulsive Boxer Uprising, which resulted in a long occupation of Peking by U.S. and Japanese forces, and persistent attempts by the big powers to split China into regional bailiwicks of foreign domination. Internally, the urgent calls to reform in the 1890s signalled the abandonment of traditional values by the intellectual elite who were only weakly opposed by a dynasty struggling to survive. The Manchu government belatedly changed its tactics and agreed to what most regionalists and western-inspired intellectuals alike both demanded— a host of political and educational reforms. In fact, this hastened its own fall. With the end of the traditional exam system in 1905 and the growth of anti-Manchu opposition as a lightening rod for disaffection, the ruling dynasty lost its legitimacy and was easily swept aside during uprisings in 1911. Popular assemblies convened across the country were not the magical solution to China's problems, however, and the next twenty-five years saw regional leaders alternately allying and struggling for power with a weak central authority. The initial surge of reform was followed by the gradual disintegration of both authority and consensus.[1]

After 1900, then, the crucial concerns of the time were not whether or not China would change but how much, in which direction, and who would guide it. Reform, *hsin fa,* was the order of the day. Accompanying the short-lived push for democratic institutions came a host of other social, political, and economic changes. Some were urged by western and Japanese powers, some were suggested by Chinese intellectuals or the progressive sectors of the local gentry, and still others were advocated by regional militarists who saw a combination of social reform and social control as the only way for China to survive. Among the unevenly implemented reforms were an attack on official corruption and anarchic banditry, the establishment of free public education, the improvement of transportation, communication, and irrigation systems, the building of factories, a ban on opium smoking, and either the suppression or control of prostitution.[2]

The reform of prostitution had long been linked with proposed changes for the treatment of women generally. By the twentieth century, most intellectuals believed that changes in women's estate were desperately needed. Their proposals ranged from a utopian vision of complete equality to more practical suggestions, such as the by now traditional appeals for an end to footbinding, female infanticide, and the disparagement of widow remarriage. But now newer and more radical demands were made for a larger female role in marriage decisions, greater freedom outside the home, and more education.

The education of women had been heatedly debated since the late eighteenth century, probably because of the increasing literacy of women under the Ch'ing and missionary-inspired notions of reform. The real impetus for change, however, came with the 1898 Reform Movement. In the face of the foreign threat to China's integrity, the elite consciously sought to alter traditional thought and institutions and enter on a path of "national reconstruction." Women's schools were established in the latter half of the nineteenth century,[3] and important intellectuals such as Liang Ch'i-ch'ao in "On Women's Education" argued for women's education not on its merits alone but as a source of national wealth and power.[4]

Few scholars and reformers publicly addressed changes in prostitution, a more problematic social role for women. One of those who did was K'ang Yu-wei, an idealistic intellectual from Canton whose proposals finally attracted attention and he was summoned to serve the government in 1898. After one hundred days of reform, his movement was brutally suppressed. K'ang's vision was as wide-ranging as it was utopian. In his *Ta t'ung shu* (*Book of Great Harmony*), written near the end of the nineteenth century but not published until 1913, K'ang outlined a program for uniting peoples and nations into one world. He sketched out those differences between classes and sexes which were to be abolished, including the oppression of women and practices such as footbinding and female infanticide. Women were to be allowed to engage in all activities and roles, and childraising was to be done communally by what he called a "human roots institution" employing women of all ages. In his new world, all adults would be equal and sex would be available to all—it would not be used to buttress inequality. He inveighed against prostitution, not because he felt sex was inherently evil, but because prostitution ensured the maintenance of women as objects and men's "playthings." He asserted that prostitution "is caused by the repressions which prevail in the age of Disorder, and when people are free to satisfy their sexual desire in a natural way, there will be no need to satisfy it in a criminal way."[5]

Other reformers lacked K'ang's unique vision. Frequently, those who openly advocated either eliminating or controlling prostitution used religious arguments which reflected their contact with western missionaries. Others appealed to the need for national reconstruction. In 1919, a Mr. B.E. Lee argued that the country was being weakened by its "fat officials, sacred members of parliament, majestic leaders of society, professed patriots, learned teachers, and opulent merchants—all of them with their 'glorious' hours in houses of ill-fame." He argued that China should be the first nation to eradicate prostitution since "we have the best women of the world in China, and if we men were but willingly to suppress prostitution we could easily accomplish it in a short time."[6]

Sidney Gamble's exhaustive work on Peking was among the more judicious of western works. He viewed prostitution as an international evil that was weakening an already threatened China. He supported the work of the reformed police and other lay organizations, as well as renewed vigilance on the part of the Christian community in China. In 1922, he bemoaned the decline of a Peking-based Social Reform Association established in 1916 to fight concubinage, prostitution, and gambling.[7]

Another survey, by western missionaries and Chinese investigators, was the Stauffer-Wong-Tewksbury report on "The Christian Occupation of China." It discussed "commercialized vice" in 71 cities and stressed the overwhelming need for reform. After detailing the reform associations and facilities existing around China, the report concluded with this pessimistic judgment: "Chinese opinion [about reform] as in other regards is incoherent and unorganized and thus generally ineffective."[8]

Most major cities had social and moral reform associations, concerned with concubinage, opium addiction, public health, aid to the handicapped, and prostitution—the same issues that concerned "progressives" from London to Chicago. Sometimes, national figures or municipal authorities were involved in these organizations, but often they were composed of private individuals. Most seem to have had uneven support and success. As in the West, the traffic in women and children was attacked by women's welfare organizations, such as the Women's Salvation Society of Canton, the Women's Rights Alliance of China, and the Chinese Anti-Kidnapping Society of Shanghai.[9] International watchdog organizations—such as the British Abolition Society's Hong Kong Anti-Mui Tsai branch and the League of Nations International Conference on the Traffic in Women and Children—began to focus on practices regarding women and their international implications.[10] In addition, state authorities instituted a few measures that made the traffic slightly more difficult: requiring each woman wishing to emigrate to be interrogated, to submit a formal request for departure, and to obtain moral and financial guarantors.

Unfortunately, these associations and reforms were more impressive on paper than in practice. The pressing demands of fiscal necessity and local administration meant that reform was more idealized than realized.

Reform, Social Order, and Control

In the early twentieth century, both the city and countryside were badly in need of new policing measures. The *pao chia*, a self-policing institution which divided the country into groups responsible for their own members, had declined in strength. Local militia and regional armies had grown in the last decades of the nineteenth century, bandit groups had proliferated, and warlord activity left parts of China disrupted and devastated.

The general consensus of the dynastic past could no longer be counted upon, and other methods had to be devised to control people, sometimes against their will, and frequently against their immediate interests as well.

In the first decades of the twentieth century, the province in which Peking was located experimented with a modern police force, both to guarantee social order and to gather political intelligence. Even before 1911, important new police measures had been implemented, including unarmed personnel, better prisons, work-houses, and other charitable facilities.[11] After the suppression of the Boxers, the United States and Japan imposed a western-style police system in Peking, believing that traditional self-policing systems could no longer be counted upon to control a divided and dislocated population.

The new police system was a fascinating amalgam of the modern and the traditional. From western organizational techniques, the Chinese borrowed methods of police distribution, specialization of functions, equipment, and training. From their own Confucian heritage, they added the importance of a moral preceptor who reminded people of the traditional consensus, mediated disputes, and assured social control. The rhetoric of police training was aimed at creating a policeman who perceived of himself as a roving "gentleman" (*chün tzu*) and appealed to Confucian principles to quell disturbances and mediate the new and often bewildering urban problems.[12]

Two factors worked against the implementation of this enlightened view. One was the low regard in which the public traditionally viewed lower officials. The whole range of sub-officialdom, usually underpaid, had often resorted to corruption, bribery, and terror to increase their power and their purse. While it was difficult for the public to view the police in a new way, there was also awareness that no one else was available to fulfill certain functions.

The result was a more ambivalent attitude laced with a great deal of distrust. The dialogue between the sing-song girl and her suitor in Chang T'ien-yi's "A Summer Night's Dream" epitomizes this ambivalence. She was convinced by her suiter that she could appeal to the police for release from her "mother," who had illegally purchased and abused her. But the owner, who had police connections, overheard the conversation, had her boyfriend chased away and had her beaten up. She then realized the police offered no hope.[13] Anecdotes in the popular press reveal that the police were expected to solve apparently insoluble urban problems—runaway wives and concubines, kidnapped daughters, conflicting accusations about debts and repayment, severe wife- or child-beatings, and fights between neighbors. The inability of the police to resolve many of these difficulties must have frustrated conscientious officers as well as the demanding public.

Another hindrance was the continuation of the connection between bullies and lower officials. This underworld received great impetus in the final years of the Ch'ing dynasty, when power devolved to local authorities who regarded the use of force as a proper tool of government.

The calls for reform and new measures for social control helped change views toward prostitution. It was now considered an evil, a "social pathology" to be controlled, not by laymen or by Christians appealing to moral instincts, but by a new police using a combination of physical force and moral suasion. But the police had interests that conflicted with this new role, and thus their attempts at control were uneven and frequently self-serving.

In 1911 the first president of the newly declared Republic, Yuan Shih-k'ai, reorganized the administration and regulation of brothels and placed them under the police. The Board of Police dealt with regulations concerning the treatment of women, taxation, health, and the maintenance of order and proper behavior. Every brothel had to register itself and its current inmates, giving the names, places of origin, and photographs of the young women. The owner had to pay a registration fee equivalent to that for opening a new store, and any changes had to be reported immediately. The police also operated a women's refuge, the Door of Hope (*Chi liang so*), as a safe retreat and retraining center for prostitutes. According to Sidney Gamble, this refuge was more a sorrowful jail than a bright haven, and its major function was to supply cheap wives for poor men, since marriage was the only way out of its halls.[14]

The Exigencies of Economics

The record of revenue exacted from brothels clearly points to a contradictory impulse working against a real reform. State income from brothels was not new; registration and taxation had been tried periodically, perhaps as early as the seventh century B.C.[15] The last years of the Ch'ing dynasty saw a revival of this practice, which endured in the early Republican period. The need to exact revenue insured the continuation of the brothel system and attempts by police to register clandestine prostitutes. Owners paid monthly charges of $3–24, depending on the level of the house. The prostitutes themselves paid an additional monthly tax of $.50–4.00, and young apprentices paid $.50–2.00. Gamble estimated that in 1924 the Peking brothels paid the government $10,967 per month or $132,000 for the year.[16] In 1913, a "major source of public income" for Canton was the tax on brothels, which, closed by reformers, were immediately reopened because of their revenue-producing potential.[17]

Feng Yü-hsiang: A Case Study in Contradictions

It has been argued that the reforms initiated in China between 1900 and 1913 were more far-reaching and more consistent than those after the final collapse of the dynasty.[18] After 1911, lip service was still paid to reform, but the disintegration of central authority meant that reforms were implemented unevenly under the control of various militarists. Significantly, most militarists included reforms for women in their new or revitalized social order.

Among the most prominent militarist-reformers was Feng Yü-hsiang, who held high posts in Chihli, Hunan, Shensi, Honan, and Inner Mongolia from 1912 to 1925. His example demonstrates one rather common approach to a controlled modernization which tried to be consistent with traditional Chinese values. His actions also throw into relief the contradictions between impulses for reform and the desire for revenue, which assured the continuing existence of prostitution.

Feng, lieutenant of a powerful northern warlord in the early 1920s, formed his own army in 1924 and struggled for control of the North. Like many other regional leaders, he was only superficially influenced by the West. Impressed by western armaments and missionaries' acts, he had converted to Christianity in 1914. He was, at bottom, a man of the people and had absorbed their basically Confucian outlook and goals. Yet, he was very much a reformer who used both moral suasion and harsh regulation to accomplish the traditional Confucian goal of providing for the people, while satisfying his own ambition for power.[19]

The contradictory nature of his goals is best seen in the area of moral reform—in his policies toward opium and prostitution. As a Christian and a Confucian moral leader, Feng vehemently opposed prostitution and prohibited his soldiers from consorting with prostitutes. Many observers erroneously assumed that he had outlawed and suppressed prostitution completely in areas under his control.[20] In fact, he merely promulgated moralistic polemics and harshly punished officers and soldiers who visited brothels. Instead of suppressing prostitution completely, he allowed it to exist discretely.

Perhaps Feng reasoned that there would always be a demand for prostitution and that brothels were the best way to observe and control prostitutes. Certainly he realized that these establishments and their inmates were one of his most lucrative sources of revenue and that even increased taxation would not diminish the demand. While establishing institutions to train prostitutes in more constructive ways of living, and opening "opium refuges" in some areas, he allowed both vices to survive under state regulation. Perhaps Feng truly wished to be the traditional "father and mother of the people." Nevertheless, he used that stance, as officials so often had, to disguise conflicting personal ambition and state interests. In the final analysis, what was most harmful to the people in the areas under Feng's control was neither opium nor prostitution, but the onerous burden of taxation he exacted. Feng's moral reforms, illustrative of the contradictions that characterized this era of transition, were as irrelevant as they were cruelly ironic.[21]

A Nation of Contradictions

After 1911, the national government was also characterized by a distance between intent and implementation, particularly in the regulation of morality. The central government, such as it was, did little for the regulation of prostitution, except to add its name to international attempts to slow down the traffic in women and children and to endorse local efforts to prevent the despoiling of young women of "good" families. The daily control and regulation of brothels, including taxation, licensing, and inspection, had always been matters for individual municipalities. Most large cities had some regulation and taxation throughout the period 1911 to 1936. Only three major cities—Chefoo, Nanking, and the Chinese settlement of Shanghai—tried consistently to prohibit prostitution, although, according to contemporary observers, with only limited success.[22] Others tried to prevent it from becoming too flagrant and exploitative, while extracting revenue from it.

Nevertheless, the national government did think it appropriate to guide public morality via the legal system. The first Republican legal code, promulgated in 1912, largely updated the Legal Code of the Ch'ing. Five areas of legislation touched on prostitution and represented the national government's attempt to prevent visible abuses: statutes referring to public disorder and immorality, the disruption of marriage and the family, health abuses, illegal procurement, and the exploitation of child labor in the guise of "adopted daughters."

Statutes on public order and morality were part of the criminal code which included sanctions against rape, pornography, and sexual relations with minors and women of "good" families. Other statutes prohibited soliciting, procuring and supplying positions for prostitutes, visiting clandestine prostitutes, singing lewd songs, exhibiting lascivious behavior in public, and remaining in teahouses after hours.[23] Statutes dealing with the protection and regulation of marriage and the family were a part of civil law. The law permitted divorce if a husband attempted or succeeded in selling his wife into prostitution and allowed concubinage, but not bigamy. Statutes attempted to keep women of good families from being used for immoral gain.[24] In the area of health, the only relevant statute.concerned abortion, which was considered a criminal act and therefore prohibited.[25]

Procuring itself was rarely mentioned in earlier codes, but it was indirectly prohibited by statutes forbidding kidnapping, immoral use of good women, and abandoning the helpless.[26] Legislation on both permanent and temporary transfers of children affected one of the prime sources of young prostitutes, the "adopted daughter." This rubric actually covered four separate conditions—slave, bondservant, adopted daughter, and adopted daughter-in-law—and was highly prone to abuse. The national government recognized that it was both powerless to prevent all transfers of children and unable to provide a more suitable alternative. As a measure of its own weakness, therefore, the government allowed the transfer of children to continue, restricting it to pawning, since this was for a limited, contracted amount of time.[27] Pawned women, at least in theory, remained part of their families.

Toward the end of the 1920s, when a national government was more firmly established in Nanking under the Kuomintang, a whole new legal code was promulgated, and many earlier reforms were enacted into law. But the government was still unable to carry them out, and, more importantly, they often conflicted with the government's desire to extract as much revenue as possible from existing vices. In 1927, slavery was legally abolished, and all "adopted daughters"—whether slaves, pawned servants, adopted daughters or daughters-in-law—were transformed into real adopted daughters before the law.[28] Of course, this was nearly impossible to implement, but it demonstrated the direction in which public and official opinion were moving. Autobiographies demonstrate that at this time, "good" families began to "liberate" those they called their slaves, although many had no recourse but to stay on as paid servants.[29] In 1928, these women were transformed into free women who could decide their own futures,[30] but the effect of this change was lessened by the reluctance of "adopted daughters," including those used as slaves, to identify themselves and the lack of public facilities to care for those who chose to leave. Restatements of this law had to be made in 1932 and again in 1936, a sure sign of ineffective legislation.[31]

A third change was increased legislation on procuring. For the first time it became a crime to make a profession of inducing women to have sexual relations for gain. An earlier prohibition of abduction and detention for immoral purposes was elaborated as well. This legislation hit poor, older women particularly hard. Yen Ching-yüeh interviewed a large number of jailed procuresses, most of whom were unaware that their occupation had been declared illegal.[32]

As with Feng Yü-hsiang's proclamations, these Nationalist statutes are more important as statements of intent than as indices of action. They had a minimal effect even in those areas under government control—particularly Central China—and practically none in other areas. The competition for control throughout most of China locked all sides in a struggle to establish and maintain sources of revenue. Thus, nearly all changes in the official treatment of prostitution were merely paper reforms.[33]

In the period 1911 to 1936, China still lacked leadership and a people dedicated to a new sense of mission and united under an ideology that took account of the old, yet promised to reshape China into a new nation. It was not yet possible, therefore, to "nationally reconstruct" China—or to abolish prostitution. Condemned in law and reviled in rhetoric, prostitution was condoned in practice and merely regulated in reality. For the transformation of its "willow lanes," China would require a revolution going well beyond the contradictory concerns with revenue and reform that shaped the Republican era.

CONCLUSION

From the middle of the nineteenth century to the 1930s, prostitution changed considerably. Contrary to the assertion of the sociologist Yen Ching-yüeh in 1934, however, it was not "utterly transformed." The sing-song girls of the early twentieth century were expected to skillfully blend the traditional with the modern. The infusion of the modern at the upper levels of the profession accounts for much of the change contemporary observers decried. Yet, they were unaware of even more fundamental changes that served to distort the institution and alter its place in Chinese society.

One major transformation occurred in procurement. In the twentieth century, as both international agencies and missionary groups discovered, purchase was giving way to pawning. During the nineteenth century, purchasers of women from destitute and desperate rural parents attempted to conceal the intended fate of the females or to use the adopted daughter fiction as a short stepping-stone to the brothels. Parents were deceived and, in the process, deprived of later income.

In the twentieth century, however, changes occurred which affected both the demand for and the supply of women. Increasing numbers of poor men sought marginal employment in cities and minimal sexual satisfaction in brothels. At the same time, there was an increase in deserted and disposed urban women, a new phenomenon—the young becoming prostitutes and the old most likely their procurers. Parents and family members reacted to these changes and to their straitened economic circumstances differently in the twentieth century. They were less likely than before to commit infanticide or sell older girls and women. Instead, they tried to maintain the fiction of the family and pawn daughters and daughters-in-law, wives and sisters, aunts and widows. Notions of filial piety forced compliance, and the families, although more tainted, shared in the profits of prostitution. After 1927, moreover, the Nationalist government gave virtually free rein to this practice.

A complementary development that buttressed the move from purchase to pawning was a transformation in mentality. Although a tainted profession, prostitution was viewed more ambivalently by the early decades of the twentieth century. Morally disapproved in both eras, its nineteenth century definition as "mean" reflected its low status and the inability of prostitutes to attain *li*. Its twentieth century label as a "social evil," on the other hand, implied that it had to be reformed and thereby cured. In order for parents to more willingly and openly traffic in their daughters' bodies, there had to be a recognition that, while prostitution may have been immoral and not respectable, it was no longer completely disreputable. Furthermore, families realized that this use of their disposable females would better insure the women's survival and therefore was preferable to infanticide or later sale.

Of prime importance, as we have seen in Peking, was the urban factor. By and large, the families who sent their daughters into prostitution in the twentieth century were urbanites who could more openly dispose of females in this fashion since they were no longer bound by traditional communities. In addition to no longer offering a moral consensus, urban centers in the early decades of the twentieth century were awash with "westernisms," especially in attitudes toward sex and relations between the sexes. Ibsen's new women profoundly challenged the Chinese view of the female, but the new-style women demonstrated the ambivalence felt by the Chinese to both this new definition and the westernisms themselves. Just as the desire for revenue militated against reform, so the ambivalence toward modern western forms prevented them from being taken too seriously.

With the benefit of hindsight, we can see that the Peking courtesan in the 1920s newspaper advertisement, photographed with telephone in hand,[34] is just a western and urban detour in the long march of Chinese social history. A more accurate reflection of underlying change, and a truer harbinger of times to come, were those Shanghai songstresses rebelling against their redefintion as common prostitutes. These women tried to roll back the historical tide by appealing to their traditional image. But they were to find that their self-image as artists was out of place in the early twentieth century— and irrelevant by its middle decades. The Chinese Revolution would bring down the final curtain on their act and on the whole system of prostitution.[35] After 1949, the leaders of a unified China began to implement a comprehensive vision of society that encompassed the liberation of women, one where politics was in command and prostitution was out of fashion. In Mao's China, there would be no traffic in sexual commodities and no place for "beautiful merchandise."

NOTES

Chapter One

1. Yü Huai, "Diverse Record of Wooden Bridge," in Howard S. Levy, *A Feast of Mist and Flowers* (Japan, 1966); Shen Fu, "Six Chapters of a Floating Life," trans. Lin Yu-t'ang *T'ien Hsia Monthly* 1 (1935): 440–52; Yü Yin-hsiang, *Dream of Green Pavilions*, discussed in Lu Hsün, *A Brief History of Chinese Fiction (Peking, 1976), pp. 319–35.

2. See Robert H. Van Gulik, *Sexual Life in Ancient China: A Preliminary Survey of Chinese Sex and Society 1500 B.C.–1644 A.D.* (Leiden, 1974), pp. 308–11; Woo Chan-cheng, *L'érotologie de la Chine* (Paris, 1963).

3. Harold Shadick, "Introduction" to Liu T'ieh-yün, *Travels of Lao Ts'an (Lao-ts'an yu-chi)* (Ithaca, 1952), pp. vii–ix; another "social" or "blame" novel is Wu Wo-yao, *Vignettes from the Late Ch'ing*, trans. Shih Shun-liu (Hong Kong, 1975).

4. From the title of Yü Huai's middle essay in Levy, *Feast*, p. 47.

5. The traditional Wade-Giles system for the romanization of Chinese words has been used throughout, largely for the readers' convenience. Most of the sources cited in the text are rendered in Wade-Giles in standard reference works and card catalogues. The use of Pinyin would have required non-specialist readers to master the conversion back to Wade-Giles; to have changed some words to Pinyin and not others was judged too confusing.

6. See, for example, E(dward) T(heodore) C(halmers) Werner, *A History of Chinese Civilization* (Shanghai, 1940), pp. 363–64; Eric Chou, *The Dragon and the Phoenix* (New York, 1970), pp. 47–66; Fernando Henriques, *Prostitution and Society: A Survey* (London, 1962), pp. 241–45; Van Gulik, *Sexual Life*, pp. 65–66, 112, 170–85; Florence Ayscough, *Chinese Women: Yesterday and Today* (Boston, 1937), pp. 92–93; Jacques Gernet, *Daily Life in China on the Eve of the Mongol Invasion: 1250–1276*, trans. H.M. Wright (Stanford, 1962), pp. 96–99.

7. Van Gulik, *Sexual Life*, pp. 170–79.

8. Gustaaf Schlegel, *Histoire de la prostitution en Chine* (Rouen, 1880), p. 6; S(amuel) Wells Williams, *The Middle Kingdom* (New York, 1883), p. 834.

9. For the following discussion, see Van Gulik, *Sexual Life*, pp. 230–35; Henriques, *Prostitution*, pp. 257–58; Schlegel, *Histoire*, pp. 8–10.

10. Chou, *Dragon*, p. 53.

11. Schlegel, *Histoire*, pp. 8–12; G. Morache, *Pékin et ses habitants: études d'hygiène* (Paris, 1869), p. 125; Liu T'ieh-yün, *Lao Ts'an*, p. 137; Henriques, *Prostitution*, p. 252.

12. Shen Fu, "Six Chapters," pp. 444–45.

13. Ibid., p. 445.

14. Ibid.; Schlegel, *Histoire*, pp. 11–12; Henriques, *Prostitution*, pp. 252–57; Chang Hsin-hai, *The Fabulous Concubine* (London, 1957), pp. 26–36.

15. Levy, *Feast*, p. 39; John Gray, *China: A History of Laws, Manners and Customs of the People* (London, 1878), p. 78.

16. Howard S. Levy, *The Illusory Flame* (Tokyo, 1962), p. 94; Gray, *China*, p. 59; J(ames) Dyer Ball, *Things Chinese* (London, 1900), p. 368.

17. Levy, *Illusory Flame*, pp. 70–78; Shen Fu, "Six Chapters," p. 443; Woo, *L'érotologie*, p. 183; Chang, *Fabulous Concubine*, pp. 28–36; Wu Ching-tze, *The Scholars (Ju-lin wai-shih)*, trans. Yang Hsien-yi and Gladys Yang (Peking, 1957), pp. 555–62.

18. Schlegel, *Histoire*, pp. 16–18; Howard Levy, *Feast*, p. 37; Morache, *Pékin*, p. 124.

19. Schlegel, *Histoire*, p. 18; Chou, *Dragon*, p. 56; Wu, *Vignettes*, p. 4.

20. Schlegel, *Histoire*, p. 23; Shen Fu, "Six Chapters," pp. 144–45.

21. Quoted in Lin Yu-t'ang, *My Country and My People* (New York, 1935), p. 161.

22. I have tried to render all figures into equivalent U.S. dollars using conversions in Albert Feuerwerker, *China's Early Industrialization* (New York, 1970), pp. 255–56. One *tael* (Haikuan or customs *tael*, Chinese *liang* or one ounce of silver) was $1.60 in 1872, $1.47 in 1877, $0.72 in 1897, and $0.63 in 1902. According to Richard Bohr, *Famine in China and the Missionary: Timothy Richards as Relief Administrator and Advocate of National Reform* (Cambridge, 1972), cash (*wen*) was a standard copper unit and in theory was 1/1000 of a silver *tael*. Ten rolls of 100 cash each were grouped together for one "string" of cash, the standard unit. The ratio of cash to *taels* varied widely among regions and individual transactions. In the spring of 1876 in North China, it was generally 1/1275–1/1500. A *yuan* or Chinese dollar during the same period was .65 *tael*.

23. Schlegel, *Histoire*, pp. 12–15; Jonathan Spence, *The Death of Woman Wang* (New York, 1978); for earlier accounts see Y(au) W(oon) Ma and Joseph Lau, *Traditional Chinese Short Stories: Theme and Variations* (New York, 1978), p. 195.

24. Wu, *Vignettes*, pp. 4, 254; Liu, *Lao Ts'an*, p. 143.

25. Ida Pruitt, *A Daughter of Han: The Autobiography of a Chinese Working Woman* (Stanford, 1967), p. 177.

26. Access to municipal, county and other governmental sources for records of taxation and licensing, of course, would give much more data in this area. At this point, these sources are not open.

27. *Chin P'ing Mei: The Adventurous History of Hsi Men and His Six Wives*, trans. by B. Miall from the German edition by Franz Kuhn (New York, 1947), p. 748, hereafter referred to as *Golden Lotus*.

28. Levy, *Feast*, p. 23.

29. Schlegel, *Histoire*, p. 37.

30. Wu, *Vignettes*, pp. 102–3, also see the anecdotes on pp. 47, 54.

31. *Golden Lotus*, pp. 65–110; Chang, *Fabulous Concubine*, pp. 37–39.

32. Such as the magistrate in Wu, *Vignettes*, p. 331, or a *Peking Gazette* article concerning a Kwangtung province military officer accused of running brothels, "a charge which it is observed, lies in general at the door of all military officials," *North China Herald*, 4 January 1877, p. 8. Also, *North China Herald* (an English language newspaper published in China), 13 July 1878, p. 36, describes an incident in the traffic of women in which "as usual, a soldier was the trader."

33. Chou, *Dragon*, pp. 54–56; Pruitt, *Daughter*, p. 71; Van Gulik, *Sexual Life*, pp. 183, 230–32, 312.

34. Guy Alitto, "Rural Elites in Transition: China's Cultural Crisis and the Problem of Legitimacy," lecture at Columbia University, 6 April 1979; *North China Herald*, 17 January 1878, p. 61; 18 January 1877, p. 65.

35. Henriques, *Prostitution*, p. 259.

36. See, Chou, *Dragon*, chaps. 7, 8 passim; Woo, *L'érotologie* for his sections on Taoism, Tantrism, chaps. 2, 3 passim, and special equipment, p. 188.

37. Schlegel, *Histoire*, pp. 13–16.

38. For discussions of this process, see ibid. and also Woo, *L'érotologie*, pp. 181–83; Howard Levy, *Feast*, p. 42; Chou, *Dragon*, pp. 50–56; Van Gulik, *Sexual Life*, pp. 178–182, 234, 285.

39. *Golden Lotus*, p. 362; Chang, *Fabulous Concubine*, p. 41.

40. Schlegel, *Histoire*, p. 20.

41. Morache, *Pékin*, p. 127; Schlegel, *Histoire*, pp. 18–19; Howard Levy, *Illusory Flame*, p. 65.

42. Morache, *Pékin*, p. 126; Wu, *Vignettes*, p. 150.

43. Van Gulik, *Sexual Life*, p. 234.

44. Morache, *Pékin*, pp. 126–27; Schlegel, *Histoire*, pp. 16–17; Wu, *Vignettes*, p. 402; Liu, *Lao Ts'an*, p. 148.

45. *Golden Lotus*, pp. 618–22, 847; Ts'ao Hsueh-ch'in, *Story of the Stone (Hung lou meng)*, trans. David Hawkes (New York, 1973), p. 301. Hereafter referred to by the more common western title, *Dream of the Red Chamber*.

46. Van Gulik, *Sexual Life*, pp. 310–12.

47. Wu, *Vignettes*, p. 254.

48. Morache, *Pékin*, pp. 127–29; Schlegel, *Histoire*, pp. 352–57.

49. Morache, *Pékin*, pp. 139–40.

50. Diana Y. Paul, *Women in Buddhism: Images of the Feminine in the Mahayana Tradition* (Berkeley, 1979), chap. 7 passim; John Blofield, *Bodhissatva of Compassion: The Mystical Tradition of Kuan Yin* (Boulder, Colorado, 1978), chap. 4 passim.

51. Pruitt, *Daughter*, p. 186; also see the remedies used in *Golden Lotus*, pp. 358, 672.

52. K'ung Shang-jen, *Peach Blossom Fan (T'ao hua-shan)*, trans. Chen Shih-hsiang and Harold Acton (Berkeley, 1976), p. 178.

53. Shen Fu, "Six Chapters," p. 445; Morache, *Pékin*, p. 125; Schlegel, *Histoire*, p.24; Chang, *Fabulous Concubine*, pp. 25–30.

54. Such as the attempts by the father to sell his daughter in Pruitt, *Daughter*, p. 69.

55. Ayscough, *Chinese Women*, pp. 95–99.

56. Woo, *L'érotologie*.

57. For example, Van Gulik, *Sexual Life*, pp. 49–50, 86, 185–200, 293–355; *Golden Lotus*, pp. 111, 189, 719; Marion Levy, *The Family Revolution in Modern China* (New York, 1971), pp. 86–87; Ts'ao, *Dream of Red Chamber*, pp. 147–50; Chou, *Dragon*, chaps. 9, 10, 11, 12 passim; Woo, *L'érotologie*.

58. As argued persuasively by Emily Ahern, "The Power and Pollution of Chinese Women" in *Women in Chinese Society*, ed. Roxane Witke and Margery Wolf (Stanford, 1975), pp. 193–214.

59. Wu in *Vignettes* clearly believes that the deterioration of late Ch'ing China was social and moral as well as economic and political; see Van Gulik's discussion of erotic late Ming art in *Sexual Life*, pp. 308–35.

60. Williams, *Middle Kingdom*, p. 834.

61. See those by Li Yü in *Li Yü's Twelve Towers*, retold by Nathan Mao (Hong Kong, 1975); Ma and Lau, *Traditional Chinese Short Stories*.

Chapter Two

1. Ch'ü T'ung-tsu, *Law and Society in Traditional China* (Paris, 1961), chap. 6 passim.

2. Ibid., pp. 24–25, 43–44, 55, 63–64, 190–98, 203–6.

3. Thomas A. Metzger, *The Internal Organization of the Ch'ing Bureaucracy* (Cambridge, 1973), pp. 185–214.

4. Kung-chuan Hsiao, *Rural China: Imperial Control in the Nineteenth Century* (Seattle, 1967), pp. 184–201; Sybille Van der Sprenkel, *Legal Institutions in Manchu China: A Sociological Analysis* (London, 1971), pp. 30–32; Ch'ü, *Law and Society,* pp. 267–79.

5. I have purposely avoided the anthropologist Robert Redfield's distinction between a Great and a Little Tradition since it fails to appreciate the complex relationship between the two sets of standards for behavior in Chinese society or the number of "little traditions" that existed. Since elite values had penetrated Chinese society to a far-reaching extent, it is difficult to make distinctions solely on the basis of class, see Old Lady Ning's general knowledge of and conservative stance on matters of propriety in Pruitt, *Daughter.*

6. *Ta Tsing Leu Lee, being the fundamental laws and selection from the supplementary statutes of the penal code of China,* trans. George T. Staunton (London, 1810; reprint ed., Taipei, 1966).

7. Ibid., pp. 79–82.

8. Ibid., p. 85.

9. Ibid., p. 110.

10. Ibid., pp. 407, 408, 410.

11. Wang Chi-men and Wu Lien-teh, *History of Chinese Medicine* (Shanghai, 1936), pp. 401–2.

12. For an interesting discussion on the changes in attitudes toward women and their *li,* see Lin Yu-t'ang, *My Country,* pp. 137–43.

13. Ayscough, *Chinese Women,* pp. 271–73, 295.

14. Spence, *Woman Wang,* p. 99.

15. Albert Richard O'Hara, *The Position of Women in Early China: According to the Lieh Nü Chuan, The Biography of Chinese Women* (Taipei, 1971), pp. 39–42.

16. Spence, *Women Wang,* p. 60.

17. Ch'ü, *Law and Society,* p. 129; according to Wolfram Eberhard, *Social Mobility in Traditional China* (Leiden, 1962), pp. 4–22, distinctions between the four Confucian social categories of free commoners were never as great as those between the legal levels of official, commoner, and mean.

18. For an estimate of the proportion of the gentry, see Chang Chung-li, *The Chinese Gentry: Studies on their Role in Nineteenth Century Chinese Society* (Seattle, 1970), p. 139.

19. For the "mean" category, see Ch'ü, *Law and Society,* pp. 128–35; see also E-tu Zen Sun and John de Francis, *Chinese Social History, Translations* (New York, 1966), pp. 142–56; Eberhard, *Social Mobility,* pp. 16–18.

20. Van Gulik, *Sexual Life,* p. 183, suggests that as early as T'ang times, only lower-class prostitution was seen as irrevocably "mean."

21. Ch'ü, *Law and Society,* pp. 187–88, 198–200, 161, argues that a double standard always existed. Elite women were absolutely forbidden to be involved with mean men, but elite males had many opportunities for intercourse with mean women, especially with slaves and prostitutes.

22. Levy, *Illusory Flame,* p. 75.

23. Wu, *Vignettes,* pp. 102–3.

24. Quoted in Henriques, *Prostitution,* p. 269.

25. For a discussion of servitude, see Ch'ü, *Law and Society,* pp. 194–98; Eberhard, *Social Mobility,* p. 17; Edouard Biot, "Memoire sur la condition des ésclaves et des serviteurs gagés en Chine," *Journal asiatique,* ser. 3, 3 (1837), pp. 246–99.

26. See the position of James L. Watson, "Chattel Slavery in Chinese Peasant Society," *Ethnology* 15 (October 1976): 361–75.

27. For the distinction between classes of people and their property, including slaves, in sumptuary laws, see Ch'ü, *Law and Society,* pp. 138–54.

28. Slavery in Chinese history is described well in Liang Ch'i-ch'ao, "Chung kuo nu li chih tu," *Ching hua hsüeh pao* 2 (December 1925): 527–53; Biot, *Memoire,* passim; Ch'ü, *Law and Society,* pp. 186–200; Eberhard, *Social Mobility,* pp. 16–17. For missionary and other western accounts, see Charles Denby, *China and Her People* (Boston, 1906), pp. 180–96, and Robert Douglas, *Society in China* (London, 1901), pp. 346–50. For an analysis of slavery in ancient China, see C(larence) Martin Wilbur, *Slavery in China during the Former Han Dynasty* (Chicago, 1943).

29. Lt. Comdr. and Mrs. Hazelwood, *Child Slavery in Hong Kong* (London, 1930); Elizabeth Andrews, *Heathen Slaves and Christian Rulers* (London, 1876). Also see J.A. Davis, *A Chinese Slave Girl* (Chicago, 1895); Lu Wheat, *The Third Daughter: A Study of Chinese Home Life* (Los Angeles, 1906); Liu, *Lao Ts'an.*

30. Pruitt, *Daughter,* p. 71.

31. Wolfram Eberhard, *Moral and Social Values of the Chinese* (Taipei, 1971), p. 206.

32. Howard S. Levy, *Monks and Nuns in a Sea of Sin,* trans. Richard F. S. Yang and Howard S. Levy (Washington, D.C., 1971); Lin Yu-t'ang, *Widow, Nun and Courtesan* (New York, 1947).

33. Wolfram Eberhard, *Sin and Guilt in Traditional China* (Berkeley, 1967), pp. 61–81. See also Tadao Sakai, "Confucianism and Popular Educational Works" in *Self and Society in Ming Thought,* ed. W(illiam) Theodore de Bary (New York, 1970), pp. 331–66.

34. Liu, *Lao Ts'an,* pp. 142–49.

35. Mao P'i-chiang, *Reminiscences of Tung Hsiao-wan,* trans. Pan Tze-yen (Shanghai, 1931); *Golden Lotus.*

Chapter Three

1. Jack Belden, *China Shakes the World* (New York, 1970), p. 277; Davis, *Slave Girl,* p. 13.

2. See H(iram) P(arkes) Wilkinson, *The Family in Classical China* (Shanghai, 1926), p. 88; Robert L. McNabb, *The Women of the Middle Kingdom* (New York, 1908), p. 15. Daughters were called "enemies" in an 1873 Hupei province proclamation against infanticide, Tsu Tu-yeu, *The Spirit of Chinese Philanthropy,* (New York, 1912), p. 57.

3. Mary Isabella Bryson, *Child Life in China* (London, 1900), p. 84; E(dward) J(ohn) Hardy, *John Chinaman at Home* (New York, 1905), p. 190; McNabb, *Women,* p. 17.

4. For those who argued it was a widespread and frequent practice, see Wilkinson, *Family,* pp. 85–93; Charles Taylor, *Five Years in China* (New York, 1860), p. 221; Robert Coltman, *The Chinese: Their Present and Future: Medical, Political and Social* (Philadelphia, 1891), p. 83; Ball, *Things Chinese,* pp. 296–98; Justice Doolittle, *Social Life of the Chinese* (New York, 1865), pp. 207–9; Arthur Smith, *Village Life in China* (New York, 1970), pp. 196–8.

For those who challenged this allegation, see J(ohn) W(illiam) Robertson-Scott, *People of China* (London, 1900), pp. 106–8; William Milne, *Life in China* (London, 1859), pp. 32–61; John Scarth, *Twelve Years in China* (Edinburgh, 1860), pp. 102–5; G. Eugène Simon, *China: Its Social, Political and Religious Life* (London, 1887), p. 22; McNabb, *Women,* p. 15.

5. Such as those issued by the treasurer of Hupei province in 1873 and a Kwang-

tung province criminal judge in 1848. Wilkinson, *Family,* p. 96; Hardy, *John China-man,* p. 191. For a translation of the 1848 edict, see Evariste Régis Huc, *Journey Through the Chinese Empire* (New York, 1859), pp. 338–39.

6. Schlegel, *Histoire,* p. 20.

7. Wong Su-ling, *Daughter of Confucius: A Personal History* (New York, 1952), pp. 47–60; Chao Pu-wei, *Autobiography of a Chinese Woman* (New York, 1947); Ts'ao, *Dream of Red Chamber,* Vol. 1.

8. Bryson, *Child Life,* pp. 94–96.

9. For a clear discussion of this murky topic, see Sophia Sa Winckler, "Family and Community in Urban Taiwan: Social Status and Demographic Strategy" (Ph.D Dissertation, Harvard University, 1975), pp. 228–38. See also Fei Hsiao-t'ung's description of the *yang hsi* tradition in *Peasant Life in China* (London, 1962), pp. 53–55.

10. For missionary women's reform work on the *mui tsai* system in Hong Kong and South China, see Elizabeth Andrews, *Heathen Slaves,* and Hazelwood, *Child Slavery.*

11. Hazelwood, *Child Slavery,* pp. 127–28.

12. Andrews, *Heathen Slaves;* Wheat, *Third Daughter;* see also McNabb, *Women,* p. 19.

13. Winckler, "Family and Community," pp. 253–70. Arthur Wolf in "Women of Haishan" in *Women in Chinese Society,* p. 98, argues that motivations for adoption were not primarily economic and that "family composition" reasons explained them better, but I would argue that these notions were still inherently economic and affected rich as well as poor families.

14. Winckler, "Family and Community," p. 239.

15. For a discussion of women's education, see Ayscough, *Chinese Women,* pp. 267–303; Isaac Headland, *Home Life in China* (New York, 1914), pp. 69–80; Evelyn Rawski, *Education and Popular Literacy in Ch'ing China* (Ann Arbor, 1979), pp. 6–8.

16. For the most detailed description of footbinding, see Howard S. Levy, *Chinese Footbinding* (New York, 1966). For later justification of the process, see Lin Yu-t'ang, *My Country,* pp. 165–69. Almost all missionary accounts included a chapter on footbinding.

17. For example, in accounts of women such as in Mao, *Reminiscences,* and Chang, *Fabulous Concubine,* and in the novels *Golden Lotus* and Li Yü, *The Before Midnight Scholar (Jou pu tuan),* trans. from the German by Richard Martin (London, 1966), usually referred to as *Prayer Mat of the Flesh.*

18. Wu, Vignettes, p. 4.

19. Hardy, *John Chinaman,* p. 14.

20. For examples of marriage negotiations and betrothal procedures, see Ayscough, *Chinese Women,* pp. 34–36; Pruitt, *Daughter,* pp. 33–34.

21. Lin, *My Country,* p. 144; Tien Tsung, "Women Who Do Not Marry," *Orient* 2 (July 1952): 41–43; Marjorie Topley, "Marriage Resistance in Rural Kwangtung" in *Studies in Chinese Society,* ed. Arthur Wolf (Stanford, 1978), pp. 247–69.

22. Lin, *My Country,* p. 148.

23. For discussions of womanhood and marriage, see Margery Wolf, "Women and Suicide," pp. 123–26; Alicia Helen Neva Bewicke Little, *Intimate China* (London, 1899); and the previously cited works by Ayscough, O'Hara, Pruitt, Belden and Hardy. There is also an extensive discussion in a little pamphlet by the Ladies' Board of Missions of the Presbyterian Church, *The Chinese Daughter-in-Law* (New York, 1875).

24. R.F. Johnson quoted in Margery Wolf, "Chinese Women: Old Skills in New Contexts" in *Women, Culture, and Society,* ed. Michelle Zimbalist Rosaldo and

Louise Lamphere (Stanford, 1974), p. 160; Hardy, *John Chinaman*, p. 196; Smith, *Village Life*, p. 231.

25. In Pruitt, *Daughter*, p. 230, Old Lady Ning attributed much of her hardship to fate and her inauspicious horoscope.

26. Ch'ü, *Law and Society*, pp. 118–23.

27. Pruitt, *Daughter*, pp. 39–47.

28. Margery Wolf in "Women and Suicide," p. 122.

29. Quoted in Hardy, *John Chinaman*, p. 196.

30. Spence, *Woman Wang*. p. 72.

31. Ibid., p. 123.

32. Pruitt, *Daughter*, p. 64.

33. Hugh Baker, *Chinese Family and Kinship* (New York, 1979), p. 168; Hsiao, *Rural China*, pp. 144–83; Tsu, *Chinese Philanthropy*. These authors counter such critics as Arthur Smith, *Chinese Characteristics* (New York, 1894; reprint ed., Port Washington, New York, 1970), pp. 194–216.

34. McNabb, *Women*, p. 47; Ayscough, *Chinese Women, p. 61.*

35. Pruitt, *Daughter*, p. 65.

36. Chang, *Fabulous Concubine*, pp. 37–39; Spence, *Woman Wang*, p. 123.

37. In fact, this was a prime argument used by journalists writing to the *North China Herald* to dispel reports of a bad famine in a locale. For example, reports about migrations from Kiangsi province in December 1876, said that since many refugee families contained wives and children, conditions could not be severe since "in bad times the Chinese pawn the first and sell the latter," 28 December 1876, p. 630.

38. Andrew Nathan, *A History of the China International Famine Relief Commission* (Cambridge, 1965), p. 1, quotes Walter Mallory that there were 1,828 famines 108 B.C. to 1911 A.D.; Alexander Hosie, that in the years A.D. 620 to 1863 there were 610 years with one or more provinces suffering from drought; and Chu Co-ching, that there were 658 floods A.D. 1–1900.

39. For descriptions of the Great North China Famine, see Bohr, *Famine and the Missionary*, pp. 13–26, and reports in the *North China Herald* especially during 1876–1878.

40. Richards, quoted in Bohr, *Famine and the Missionary*, pp. 18–19. See also p. 21.

41. Tseng Kuo-ch'uan, quoted in Bohr, *Famine and the Missionary*, p. 23.

42. Rev. DiMarchi, "Letter" in *North China Herald*, 14 July 1877, p. 40.

43. DiMarchi, "Letter"; Timothy Richards, reported in *Forty-Five Years in China* (London, 1916), p. 132, that "he saw only seven persons today, but no woman was among them." The number, of course, was diminished as much by the malnutrition and maltreatment of women as by their sale.

44. For example, Letter to the *North China Herald*, 29 June 1878, pp. 673, 677, remarked on an orphanage near Tientsin with 20 boys and 100 girls; another of 27 July 1878, pp. 89–90, spoke of one with 70 girls and 55 boys.

45. T. Richards, article in the *North China Herald*, 21 March 1878, pp. 296–98.

46. Richards, *Forty-five Years*, p. 118.

47. Ibid., p. 132; Wu, Vignettes, p. 331.

48. For a discussion of how the marriage market affected poor men, see Marion Levy, *Family Revolution*, pp. 17, 118. The theme of a man meeting his intended in a brothel was common in realistic novels of the early twentieth century, see Hsia Tsi-an, *Gate of Darkness* (Seattle, 1968), p. 93.

49. Ayscough, *Chinese Women*, p. 258.

50. *North China Herald*, 11 May 1878, p. 492.

51. Spence, *Woman Wang*, p. 105; Wheat, *Third Daughter*, p. 154.

52. Denby, *China;* McNabb, *Women,* p. 19.
53. Spence, *Woman Wang,* p. 105.
54. Schlegel, *Histoire,* p. 19; H. Levy, *Illusory Flame,* p. 75; Wu, *Vignettes,* p. 191.
55. Schlegel, *Histoire,* pp. 21–23; Arnold Foster, Letter from Shansi province to *North China Herald,* 15 November 1877, p. 457.
56. McNabb, *Women,* p. 19.
57. Pruitt, *Daughter,* p. 69; Liu, *Lao Ts'an,* p. 158; Pruitt, *Daughter,* p. 168. For other citations, see the *North China Herald,* 13 July 1878, p. 36; *Golden Lotus,* p. 791; Wu, *Vignettes,* p. 154.
58. Wu, *Vignettes,* p. 331.
59. Levy, *Feast,* pp. 42, 50–56; Wu, *Vignettes.*
60. Igor Kopytoff and Suzanne Miers, "African 'Slavery' as an Institution of Marginality" in their *Slavery in Africa: Historical and Anthropological Perspectives* (Madison, 1977), p. 12. See also in the same volume, Gerald Hartwig, "The Changing Face of Servitude Among the Kerabe of Tanzania," p. 269.
61. Annette Wiener, *Women of Value, Men of Renown* (Houston, 1974).

Chapter Four

1. J. Lemière, "Sing Song Girl: From a Throne of Glory to a Seat of Ignominy," *China Journal of Science and Art* 1 (March 1923): 126–30.
2. Yen Ching-yüeh, "Crime in Relation to Social Change in China" (Ph.D. Dissertation, University of Chicago, 1936), pp. 101–2.
3. Literature in the teens and early twenties tended to focus on the romantic plight of modern urban youth, but in the late twenties and thirties a self-consciously "proletarian literature" portraying the plight of the rural and urban masses developed. Prostitutes and courtesans figure prominently in this fiction.
4. Andrew Nathan, *Peking Politics 1918–23* (Berkeley, 1976), pp. xv–xvii; F(ook-lam) Gilbert Chan and Thomas H. Etzold, eds. *China in the 1920s* (New York, 1976), pp. 2–4.
5. Sidney Gamble, *Peking: A Social Survey* (New York, 1922), p. 257.
6. Such as Chang T'ien-yi, "Smile" and "Reunion" in *Contemporary Chinese Stories,* trans. and ed. Chi-chen Wang (New York, 1944), pp. 108–17, 119–26.
7. *La vie populaire à Pékin (d'après la presse chinoise)* (Peking, 1926), p. 192. This source, a French translation of human interest items from Chinese newspapers, is very useful.
8. James Sheridan, *Chinese Warlord: The Career of Feng Yü-hsiang* (Stanford, 1966), p. 246, for a list of various surcharges in Amoy; pp. 156–57, 206, 248–50, 287, to trace Feng's increasingly desperate grasp for funds.
9. J(ean) J(acques) Matignon, *La Chine hermétique: superstitions, crime et misère* (Paris, 1936), pp. 259–62.
10. Much of the debate about peasant immiseration still centers around Ramon Myers, *Chinese Peasant Economy: Agricultural Development in Hopei and Shantung, 1890–1949* (Cambridge, 1970). See Also Dwight Perkins, *Agricultural Development in China: 1368–1968* (Chicago, 1969); R(ichard) H(enry) Tawney, *Land and Labor in China* (London, 1927).
11. League of Nations, "Report of the Commission of Enquiry into Traffic in Women and Children in the East," New York, 1933, p. 40.
12. Olga Lang, *Chinese Family and Society* (New Haven, 1946), p. 126; see page 151 for a table comparing male and female population ratios compiled by Buck and others.

13. Lao She, *Rickshaw Boy*, trans. Evan King (New York, 1945), p. 60.

14. For example, Old Lady Ning in Pruitt, *Daughter*, p. 71.

15. Jean Chesneaux, *The Chinese Labor Movement*, trans. H. M. Wright (Stanford, 1968), pp. 95–97, 110–11.

16. Lao She, *Rickshaw Boy*, pp. 271, 294.

17. Margery Wolf, *House of Lim* (Englewood Cliffs, N.J., 1968). See Jou Shih, "Slave Mother," trans. George Kennedy in *Straw Sandals*, ed. Harold Isaacs (Cambridge, 1974), pp. 215–41, for a slightly different use of pawning.

18. League of Nations, "Report," pp. 44, 141; Chang T'ien-yi, "A Summer Night's Dream," trans. Sidney Shapiro, *Chinese Literature* no. 1 (1962), pp. 3–26.

19. Martin C. Yang, *Chinese Social Structure* (Taipei, 1969), pp. 245–413. There has been an enormous increase in the literature on elites in Republican China. Much of it, however, focuses on one type of elite, e.g. political elites, or on one locality. See Chang P'eng-yuan, "Political Participation and Political Elites in Early Republican China: The Parliament of 1913–14," *Journal of Asian Studies* 37 (February 1978): 293–313; Keith Schoppa, "Local Self Government in Chekiang 1909–27," *Modern China* 2(October 1976): 503–27; Mary Backus Rankin, "Leading Families in Two Chekiang Marketing Towns," *Ch'ing shih wen-t'i* 3 (November 1977), pp. 67–104.

20. Yang, *Social Structure*, pp. 253–67.

21. Ibid., pp. 269–84.

22. Yet, even the new generation, as Chang P'eng-yuan argues in "Political Participation," p. 300, were "at most quasi-modern and quasi-traditional."

23. Yang, *Social Structure*, pp. 296–315; Schoppa, "Local Self Government," pp. 524–25.

24. Yang, *Social Structure, pp. 316–25*

25. Lang, *Family*, p. 224.

26. Leo Ou-fan Lee, *The Romantic Generation of Chinese Writers* (Cambridge, 1973), p. 275.

27. Yang, *Social Structure*, p. 282.

28. Ts'ao Yü, "The History of Drama in Modern China," lecture at Columbia University, 27 March 1980.

29. Lang, *Family*, p. 95.

30. E(ugene) Perry Link, "The Rise of Modern Popular Fiction in Shanghai" (Ph.D. Dissertation, Harvard University, 1976), pp. 110–13.

31. Lao She, "A Vision," trans. Gladys Yang, *Chinese Literature*, no. 6 (1962), pp. 77–88; *Rickshaw Boy*, p. 321.

32. As pointed out both by Perry Link, "Modern Popular Fiction," pp. 275–341, and Leo Lee, *Romantic Generation*. pp. 275–79.

33. "Cultural imperialism" has been defined as the spread of the ideology of a dominant culture, with the emulation and substitution of foreign cultural forms for the native culture. See Science for the People, "Science as Cultural Imperialism" in *Communication and Class Struggle*, vol. 1 *Capitalism and Imperialism*, Armand Mattelart and Seth Sigeluart, eds. (New York, 1979).

34. Shirley Garrett, "The Chambers of Commerce and the Y.M.C.A." in *The Chinese City Between Two Worlds*, ed. G(eorge) William Skinner and Mark Elvin (Stanford, 1974), p. 213.

35. Rhoads Murphy, "Treaty Ports and China's Modernization" in *Chinese City*, p. 33.

36. Fei Hsiao-t'ung, "Relation Between City and Village in China," *China Economist* 2 (15 November 1948): 138–39, 149.

37. Gamble, *Peking*, pp. 102–8.

38. Ibid., pp. 94, 110–11.

39. Lang, *Family*, pp. 81–101.

40. Garret, "Chambers of Commerce," pp. 214–25.

41. In his study of another North China city, David Buck concluded that the gap between westernizing elites and the people prevented China from changing. *Urban Change in China* (Madison, 1978), p. 215.

42. Lang, *Family*, p. 79.

43. Gamble, *Peking*, pp. 38, 270; police survey quoted in Lamson, *Social Pathology*, p. 14.

44. Gamble, *Peking*, p. 99.

45. Ibid., pp. 102–3, 105–6.

46. David Strand, "Streetcar Conductors, Rickshaw Pullers, and Policemen: Peking in the 1920's," lecture at Columbia University, 24 April 1979.

47. Lang, *Family*, p. 80.

48. Gamble, *Peking*, pp. 109–10.

49. Ibid., pp. 255–56.

50. Sherman Cochran, *Big Business in China: Sino-Foreign Rivalry in the Cigarette Industory: 1890–1930* (Cambridge, 1980), p. 70.

51. Gamble, *Peking*, p. 246; *She hui t'ung chi* (*Social Statistics*) no. 54 (14 July 1930); pp. 5–6.

Chapter Five

1. Gamble, *Peking*, pp. 247–8; Robert Swallow, *Sidelights on Peking Life* (Peking, 1927), pp. 31–44; Lewis C. Arlington and William Lewisohn, *In Search of Old Peking* (Peking, 1935), pp. 272–74.

2. Gamble, *Peking*, p. 427.

3. Ibid.

4. Ts'ao Yü "Sunrise," trans. A.D. Barnes (Peking, 1960).

5. As always, there is a problem in translating these terms into English. This category does not exactly correspond to the western "streetwalker," but for lack of a better term I have used it for women in unlicensed houses who solicited more openly.

6. Lao She, "Crescent Moon," trans. Sidney Shapiro, *Chinese Literature*, no. 4 (1957), pp. 66–88.

7. Lao She, *Rickshaw Boy*, pp. 265–77, 294.

8. According to a report by Milton Stauffer with T(sin-forn C.) Wong and M. Gardner Tewskbury, *The Christian Occupation of China: A General Survey of the Numerical Strength and Geographical Distribution of the Christian Forces in China Made by the Special Committee on Survey and Occupation of China Continuation Committee, 1918-21* (Shanghai, 1922), p. 396, 46 percent of the respondents cited no open solicitation in their cities, 37 percent said some, and 17 percent reported little. This report was a valuable survey conducted by missionaries polling their representatives in cities across China.

9. League of Nations, "Report," p. 139.

10. *La vie populaire* (1923), p. 9; (1926), p. 309; (1925), p. 103. One of the "sisters" in Chang's "Dream" was supporting her family.

11. This sister in Chang's "Dream" wished she had been purchased rather than pawned. It is implied that she was even prohibited from marrying since then her family would be deprived of vital income.

12. See Shen Tseng-wen, "The Husband" in *The Chinese Earth*, trans. and ed. Chang Ti and Robert Payne (London, 1947), pp. 41–60; Yen, "Crime," p. 91; Margery Wolf, *House of Lim*, p. 102.

13. *North China Herald*, 23 October 1920, pp. 231–32; 13 November 1920, p. 465.

14. Lemière, "Sing Song Girl," p. 130.
15. *La vie populaire* (1922), p. 6; (1925), p. 122; (1924), p. 218; (1925), p. 174; (1926), pp. 178–79. Also see Yen, chap. 4 passim, for his descriptions of poor city women tricked into prostitution.
16. Peking United International Famine Relief Committee, *North China Famine 1920–1 with Special Reference to the West Chihli Area* (Peking, 1922), p. 87.
17. Lao She, *Rickshaw Boy*, p. 265.
18. Such as poor rural children whose parents were working in nearby fields, and poor women working on the street such as those sewing coolies' clothing. See *La vie populaire* (1926), p. 406.
19. Yen, "Crime," pp. 72–80.
20. Myers, *Peasant Economy*, especially pp. 276–95.
21. Mallory, *Land of Famine;* Famine Relief Committe, *North China Famine*, pp. 14–15; North China International Society of Famine Relief, *Final Report in Connection with the Famine of 1920–1* (Tientsin, 1921); Nathan, *China International Famine Relief Commission*, p. 2.
22. North China International Society, *Final Report*, pp. 7–9; Famine Relief Committee, *North China Famine*, pp. 14, 59, 87–92.
23. Famine Relief Committee, *North China Famine*, p. 89.
24. Hsiao Kan, "Return to Daylight: the Reformation of Peking Prostitutes," *People's China* 1 (March 1950): 22; *La vie populaire* (1922), p. 76; *North China Herald*, 23 October 1920, p. 228; 25 December 1920, p. 865.
25. League of Nations, "Report," p. 62.
26. Ibid.
27. Yen, "Crime," pp. 88–89.
28. League of Nations, "Report," pp. 138–39.
29. Yen, "Crime," pp. 86–90.
30. Hsiao Kan, "Return to Daylight," p. 25.
31. Gamble, *Peking*, p. 250.
32. Lao She, "Crescent Moon," p. 86.
33. Chang, "Dream;" see also *La vie populaire* (1925), p. 348; Hsiao Kan, "Return to Daylight."
34. Herbert Lamson, "Family Limitation Among Educated Chinese Married Women," *Chinese Medical Journal* 47 (1937): 493–503, found that in 1928 only 20 of 120 college educated women had any knowledge of modern contraception, although all agreed it was important to limit births. However, Olga Lang in *Family*, p. 153, suggests that many of the "native" methods were quite successful in limiting births.
35. J. Preston Maxwell, "On Criminal Abortion in China," *China Medical Journal* 42 (1928): 12–19; Matignon, *Chine hermétique*, pp. 259–62.
36. See Dr. Lai, "Syphilis and Prostitution in Kiangsu," *China Medical Journal* 44 (1930): 558–63; Lamson, *Social Pathology*, p. 363.
37. Quoted in Lamson, *Social Pathology*, p. 354; see also Dr. Korns, "Examination of Domestic Servants for Communicable Diseases," *China Medical Journal* 34 (1920): 624–29; Dr. Heimburger, "The Incidence of Syphilis at the Shantung Christian University Dispensary," *China Medical Journal* 41 (1927): 541–50. Note, however, that these were usually people checking into western clinics for other health problems and do not represent a cross section of the population.
38. Lamson, *Social Pathology*, p. 356.
39. Lao She, "Crescent Moon," pp. 86–87; "Vision," pp. 77–88.
40. Chang, "Dream."
41. Ts'ao Yü, "Sunrise," pp. 135–36; see also *La vie populaire* (1926), p. 41.
42. Lao She, *Rickshaw Boy*, pp. 234–37, is a vivid description of one such poor courtyard.

Chapter Six

1. For example, James Sheridan, *China in Disintegration* (New York, 1975); Mary C. Wright, "Introduction," *China in Revolution: the First Phase 1900–1913* (New Haven, 1968), pp. 1–63; Kwang-ching Liu, "Nineteenth Century China: Disintegration of the Old Order and Impact of the West," in *China in Crisis,* ed. Ho P'ing-ti and Tang Tsou, (Chicago, 1968), pp. 93–178.

2. Sheridan, *Chinese Warlord,* pp. 104–5, 113–14.

3. Meribeth Cameron, *The Reform Movement in China 1898–1912* (New York, 1967), pp. 83–84; Linda Shin, "Women and Reform" in *Reform in Nineteenth Century China,* ed. Paul Cohen and John Schrecker (Cambridge, 1976), pp. 245–51.

4. Joanna Handlin, "Lu K'un's New Audience" in *Women in Chinese Society,* pp. 36–38; Mary Backus Rankin, "The Emergence of Women at the End of the Ch'ing" in *Women in Chinese Society,* pp. 39–45. Also see Sophia H. Chen Zen, ed. *Symposium on Chinese Culture,* especially P.S. Tseng, "The Chinese Woman, Past and Present" (New York, 1931, reprint ed. New York, 1969), pp. 281–92. As Mary Rankin points out in "Emergence of Women," p. 64, the "liberation" of Chinese women was rarely argued on its own terms, but rather in terms of other issues, for example, whether it would add to China's wealth and power, to its national strength versus Japan, to making China whole again, or would help make revolution and defeat feudal forces.

5. *Ta t'ung shu: the One World Philosophy of K'ang Yu-wei,* trans. with notes Lawrence Thompson (London, 1968), pp. 251, 248–53, 187–95, 149–68.

6. B.E. Lee, "How Can We Honor Chinese Women," *Chinese Recorder* (October 1919): 663–64.

7. Gamble, *Peking,* p. 263.

8. Stauffer, "Christian Occupation," p. 397.

9. League of Nations, "Report," pp. 156–57, 160.

10. Ray Everett, "International Traffic in Women and Children," *Journal of Social Hygiene* 13 (May 1927): 269–76.

11. Steve MacKinnon, "Police Reform in Late Ch'ing Chihli," *Ch'ing shih wen-t'i* 3 (1979): 82–99.

12. David Strand, "Conductors, Pullers, and Policemen" lecture.

13. Chang, "Dream," p. 19.

14. Gamble, *Peking,* pp. 248–49; 476–85; League of Nations, "Report," pp. 133–38.

15. Van Gulik, *Sexual Life,* pp. 65–66.

16. Gamble, *Peking,* p. 480.

17. Garrett, "Chambers of Commerce," p. 215.

18. Mary Wright, *China in Revolution,* pp. 1–63.

19. Sheridan, *Chinese Warlord,* pp. 284–88.

20. Ibid.

21. Ibid., pp. 92, 158, 245–49, fn 69, p. 323, fn 34, p. 338.

22. League of Nations, "Report," p. 133.

23. *The Chinese Criminal Code and Special Criminal and Administrative Laws,* trans. and annotated by Legal Department of Shanghai Municipal Council (Shanghai, 1935), pp. 81–84, 162–66, 173–74.

24. V(alentin) A(lexandrovich) Riasanovsky, *The Modern Civil Law of China* (Harbin, 1927), pp. 148, 135.

25. *Chinese Criminal Code,* pp. 104–5.

26. Ibid., pp. 106, 126–27.

27. Riasanovsky, *Civil Law,* p. 122.

28. League of Nations, "Report," p. 132.

29. For example, Wong, *Daughter of Confucius*, p. 301.

30. League of Nations, "Report," pp. 160–63.

31. "The Mui Tsai System in China, Hong Kong, and Malaya," *International Labour Review* 34 (November 1936): 663–76.

32. According to Yen, "Crime," p. 47, 71 percent of the women over 50 years of age who had been arrested were charged with abduction or kidnapping. He calls these "economic crimes" since they were actions necessary to ensure survival and represented a traditional practice—old women obtaining slave girls for sale—that had become illegal in its new guise—kidnapping young women for prostitution.

33. Lloyd Eastman, *The Abortive Revolution: China Under Nationalist Rule 1927–1937* (Cambridge, 1974).

34. As shown in Gamble, *Peking,* p. 254.

35. A fascinating article by Chi-hsi Hu, 'The Sexual Revolution in the Kiangsi Soviet," *China Quarterly* 59 (July-September 1974): 477–90, examines the evolution of this attitude and the initial experiments with greater sexual freedom in the Chinese Communist Party policies of the 1930s.

BIBLIOGRAPHY

Primary Sources

Newspapers

North China Herald and Supreme Court Gazetteer, Shanghai, 17–21 (1876–78); 136 (1920); 137 (1920).

Chinese Biographies in English

Chao Pu-wei. *Autobiography of a Chinese Woman*. New York, 1947.
Chiang Yee. *A Chinese Childhood*. London, 1963.
Lin Yu-t'ang. *My Country and My People*. New York, 1935.
McAleavy, Henry, trans. *That Chinese Woman: The Life of Sai Chin-hua*. New York, 1959.
Mao P'i-chiang. *The Reminiscences of Tung Hsiao-wan*. Translated by Pan Tze-yen. Shanghai, 1931.
Pruitt, Ida. *A Daughter of Han: The Autobiography of a Chinese Working Woman*. Stanford, 1967.
Shen Fu. "Six Chapters of a Floating Life." Translated by Lin Yu-t'ang. *T'ien Hsia Monthly* 1 (1935): 440–52.
Wong Su-ling. *Daughter of Confucius: A Personal History*. New York, 1952.
Yü Huai. "Diverse Records of Wooden Bridge." In *A Feast of Mist and Flowers: The Gay Quarters of Nanking at the End of the Ming*. Translated and annotated by Howard S. Levy. Tokyo 1966.

Nineteenth and Twentieth Century Contemporary Accounts of China

Physicians

Coltman, Robert, Jr. *The Chinese: Their Present and Future: Medical, Political, Social*. Philadelphia, 1891.
Everett, Ray. "International Traffic in Women and Children." *Journal of Social Hygiene* 13 (May 1927): 269–76.
Fearn, Ann. *My Days of Strength: An American Woman Doctor's Forty Years in China*. New York, 1939.
Gervais, Albert. *Medicine Man in China*. Translated by Vincent Sheean. New York, 1934.
Heimburger, Dr. "The Incidence of Syphilis at the Shantung Christian University Dispensary." *China Medical Journal* 41 (1927): 541–50.
Hume, Edward H. *The Chinese Way in Medicine*. Baltimore, n.d.
Korns, Dr. "An Examination of Domestic Servants for Communicable Diseases." *China Medical Journal* 34 (1920): 624–29.
Lai, Dr. "Syphillis and Prostitution in Kiangsu." *China Medical Journal* 44 (1930): 558–63.

Lamson, Herbert. "Family Limitation Among Educated Married Women." *China Medical Journal* 47 (1933): 493–503.
Lockhart, William. *The Medical Missionary in China: A Narrative of Twenty Years of Experience.* London, 1861.
Matignon, J(ean) J(acques). *La Chine hermétique: superstitions, crime et misère.* Paris, 1936.
Maxwell, J. Preston. "On Criminal Abortion in China." *China Medical Journal* 42 (1928): 251–62.
Morache, G. *Pékin et ses habitants: études d'hygiène.* Paris, 1869.
"The Social Evil in China." *China Medical Journal* 34 (1920): 635–37.
Taylor, Charles. *Five Years in China: With an Account of the Great Rebellion and a Description of St. Helena.* New York, 1860.
Wong, K.C. "The Social Evil in China." *China Medical Journal* 34 (1920): 630–34.
Wu Lieh-teh. "The Problem of Venereal Disease in China." *China Medical Journal* 41 (1927): 28–35.

Missionaries, Diplomats, Travellers, Chinese and Western Social Surveys

American Red Cross China Famine Relief Committee. *Report of the China Famine Relief American Red Cross October 1920–September 1921.*
Andrews, Elizabeth. *Heathen Slaves and Christian Rulers.* London 1876.
Arlington, L(ewis) C(harles) and Lewisohn, William. *In Search of Old Peking.* Peking, 1935.
Ayscough, Florence. *Chinese Women: Yesterday and Today.* Boston, 1937; reprint ed., New York, 1975.
Ball, J(ames) Dyer. *Things Chinese: Being Notes on Various Subjects Connected with China.* London, 1900.
Biot, Edouard. "Memoire de la condition des ésclaves et des serviteurs gagés en Chine." *Journal asiatique.* ser. 3, 3 (1837), pp. 246–99.
Bryson, Mary Isabella. *Child Life in China.* London, 1900.
Buck, John Lossing. *Land Utilization in China.* Nanking, 1937.
Central China Famine Relief Committee. *Report and Accounts from October 1, 1900–June 30, 1912.* Shanghai, 1912.
Denby, Charles. *China and Her Peoples: Being the Observations, Reminiscences and Conclusions of an American Diplomat.* Boston, 1906.
Doolittle, Justus. *Social Life of the Chinese: With Some Accounts of the Religious, Governmental, Educational, and Business Customs and Opinions.* New York, 1865; reprint ed., Taipei, 1966.
Douglas, Robert. *Society in China.* London, 1901.
Gamble, Sidney. *Peking: A Social Survey.* New York, 1922.
Gray, John Henry. *China: A History of Laws, Manners and Customs of the People.* London, 1878.
Hardy, Edward John. *John Chinaman at Home: Sketches of Men, Manners, and Things in China.* New York, 1905.
Hazelwood, Lt. Cmdr. and Mrs. *Child Slavery in Hong Kong.* London, 1930.
Headland, Isaac Taylor. *Home Life in China.* New York, 1914.
Hodous, Lewis. *Folkways in China.* London, 1929.
Holcombe, Chester. *The Real Chinaman.* New York, 1895.
Hsiao Kan. "Return to Daylight: Reforming Peking Prostitutes." *People's China* 1 (March 1950): 12–26.

Huc, Evariste Régis. *A Journey Thrugh the Chinese Empire*. New York, 1859.

Ladies' Board of Missions of the Presbyterian Church. *Chinese Daughter-in-Law*. New York, 1875.

Lamson, Herbert. *Social Pathology in China*. Shanghai, 1934.

Lay, G. Tradescent. *The Chinese as They Are: Moral, Social and Literary Characteristics*. London, 1841.

Lang, Olga. *Chinese Family and Society*. New Haven, 1946.

Lee, B.E. "How Can We Honor Chinese Women?" *Chinese Recorder* (October 1919): 663–64.

League of Nations. Report of the Commission of Enquiry into the Traffic in Women and Children in the East. New York, 1933.

Lemière, J. "Sing Song Girl: From a Throne of Glory to a Seat of Ignominy." *Chinese Journal of Sociology and Anthropology* 1 (March 1923): 126–130.

Little, Alicia Helen Neva Bewicke. *Intimate China: The Chinese As I have Seen Them*. London, 1899.

Lo, R(en) Y(en). *The Opium Problem in the Near East*. Shanghai, 1933.

McClory, Thomas. "Is Slavery as Practiced by the Chinese Immoral?" *Chinese Recorder and Missionary Journal* 22 (1891): 567–73.

McNabb, Robert L. *Women of the Middle Kingdom*. New York, 1908.

Mallory, Walter. *China: Land of Famine*. New York, 1926.

Milne, William C. *Life in China: Fourteen Years Among the Chinese*. London, 1859.

"Mui Tsai System in China, Hong Kong, and Malaya." *International Labour Review* 34 (November 1936): 663–76.

Nevius, Helen. *The Life of John Livingston Nevius*. New York, 1895.

North China International Society for Famine Relief. *Final Report in Connection with the Famine of 1920–1*. Tientsin, 1921.

Peking United International Famine Relief Committee. *North China Famine of 1920–21 with Special Reference to the West Chihli Area*. Peking, 1922.

Richards, Timothy. *Forty-five Years in China: Reminiscences*. London, 1910.

Robertson-Scott, J(ohn) W(illiam). *The People of China: Their Country, History Life, Ideas and Relations with the Foreigner*. London, 1900.

Scarth, John. *Twelve Years in China: The People, the Rebels, and the Mandarins*. Edinburgh, 1860.

Simon, G. Eugène. *China: Its Social, Political, and Religious Life*. London, 1887.

Smith, Arthur H. *Chinese Characteristics*. New York, 1894; reprint ed., Port Washington, New York, 1970.

———. *Village Life in China*. New York, 1899; reprint ed., New York, 1970.

Stauffer, Milton, Wong, T(sin-forn C.), and Tewksbury, M. Gardner. *The Christian Occupation of China: A General Survey of the Numerical Strength and Geographical Distribution of the Christian Forces in China Made by the Special Committee on Survey and Occupation of China Continuation Committee, 1918–21*. Shanghai, 1922.

Swallow, Robert. *Sidelights on Peking Life*. Peking, 1927.

Tawney, R(ichard) H(enry). *Land and Labor in China*. London, 1927.

Tseng, P.S. "The Chinese Woman, Past and Present." In *Symposium on Chinese Culture*. Edited by Sophia H. Chan Zen. New York, 1931, reprint ed., New York, 1969, pp. 281–92.

La vie populaire à Pékin (d'après la presse chinoise). Pékin, 1922, 1923, 1924, 1925, 1926, 1927.

Wieger, Leon. *Moral Tenets and Customs in China*. Hokien Fu, 1913.

Williams, S(amuel) Wells. *The Middle Kingdom*. New York, 1883.

Yen Ching-yüeh. "Crime in Relation to Social Change in China." Ph.D. Dissertation, University of Chicago, 1934.

Literary Works

Chang Hsin-hai. *The Fabulous Concubine.* London, 1957.

Chang T'ien-yi. "A Summer Night's Dream." Translated by Sidney Shapiro. *Chinese Literature,* no. 1 (1962), pp. 3–26.

———. "Reunion." In *Contemporary Chinese Stories.* Edited and translated by Chi-chen Wang. New York, 1944, pp. 119–26.

———. "Smile." in *Contemporary Chinese Stories.* Edited and translated by Chi-chen Wang. New York, 1944, pp. 108–17.

Chin P'ing Mei: The Adventurous History of Hsi Men and His Six Wives (usually translated as *Golden Lotus*). Translated by B. Miall from the German edition by Franz Kuhn. New York, 1947.

Davis, J.A. *The Chinese Slave Girl: A Story of Women's Life in China.* Chicago, 1895.

Jou Shih. "Slave Mother." Translated by George Kennedy. In *Straw Sandals.* Edited by Harold Isaacs. Cambridge, 1974, pp. 215–41.

K'ung Shang-jen. *Peach Blossom Fan (T'ao hua shan).* Translated by Shih-hsiang Chen and Harold Acton. Berkeley, 1976.

Kyn Yn Yu, J.B. *The Tragedy of Ah Qin and Other Modern Chinese Stories.* New York, 1931.

Lao She. "Crescent Moon." Translated by Sidney Shapiro. *Chinese Literature,* no. 4 (1957), pp. 66–88.

———. *Rickshaw Boy.* Translated by Evan King. New York, 1945.

———. "A Vision." Translated by Gladys Yang. *Chinese Literature,* no. 6 (1962), pp. 77–88.

Li Yü's Twelve Towers. Retold by Nathan Mao. Hong Kong, 1975.

Lin Yu-t'ang. *Widow, Nun and Courtesan.* New York, 1947.

Liu T'ieh-yün. *The Travels of Lao Ts'an (Lao-ts'an yu-chi).* translated by Harold Shadick. Ithaca, 1971.

Levy, Howard S. *The Illusory Flame: Translations from the Chinese.* Tokyo, 1962.

———. *Monks and Nuns in a Sea of Sin.* Translated by Richard F. S. Yang and Howard S. Levy. Washington, D.C., 1971.

Ma, Y(au) W(oon), and Lau, Joseph. *Traditional Chinese Short Stories: Theme and Variations.* New York, 1978.

Shen Tsung-wen. *The Chinese Earth.* Translated by Chang Ti and Robert Payne. London, 1947.

Ta t'ung shu: The One World Philosophy of K'ang Yu-wei. Translated and with notes by Lawrence Thompson. London, 1968.

Ts'ao Hsüeh-ch'in. *The Story of the Stone (Hung lou meng,* usually translated as *Dream of the Red Chamber).* Translated by David Hawkes. New York, 1973.

Ts'ao Yü. "Sunrise." Translated by A.C. Barnes. Peking, 1960.

Wang Shih-fu. *Romance of the Western Chamber (Hsi-hsiang chi).* Translated by Shih I Hsiung. New York, 1968.

Wheat, Lu. *The Third Daughter: A Story of Chinese Home Life.* Los Angeles, 1906.

Wu Ching-tze. *The Scholars (Ju-lin wai-shih).* Translated by Yang Hsien-yi and Gladys Yang. Peking, 1957.

Wu Wo-yao. *Vignettes from the Late Ch'ing.* Translated by Shih Shun-liu. Hong Kong, 1976.

Law Codes in English Translation

Chinese Criminal Code and Special Criminal and Administrative Laws. Translated and annotated by the Legal Department of Shanghai Municipal Council. Shanghai, 1935.

Riasanovsky, V(alentin) A(lexandrovich).*The Modern Civil Code of China*. Harbin, 1927.

Ta Tsing Leu Lee. Being the fundamental laws and selection from the supplementary statutes of the penal code of China. Translated by George T. Staunton. London, 1810; reprint ed., Taipei, 1966.

Secondary Sources

Western and Chinese Scholarly Works on Chinese Society

Ahern, Emily. "Power and Pollution of Chinese Women." In *Studies in Chinese Society,* edited by Arthur Wolf. Stanford, 1978, pp. 269–90.

Baker, Hugh. *Chinese Family and Kinship*. New York, 1979.

Balaczs, Etienne. *Chinese Civilization and Bureaucracy: Variations on a Theme*. Translated by H.M. Wright. New Haven, 1964.

Belden, Jack. *China Shakes the World*. New York, 1970.

Blofield, John. *Bodhissatva of Compassion: The Mystical Tradition of Kuan Yin*. Boulder, Colorado, 1978.

Bohr, Paul Richard. *Famine in China and the Missionary: Timothy Richards as Relief Administrator and Advocate of National Reform*. Cambridge, 1972.

Cameron, Meribeth. *The Reform Movement in China, 1898–1912*. New York, 1967.

Chan, F(ook-lam) Gilbert, and Etzold, Thomas E., eds. *China: the 1920's*. New York, 1976.

Chang Chung-li. *The Chinese Gentry: Studies on Their Role in Nineteenth Century China*. Seattle, 1970.

Chang P'eng-yuan. "Political Participation and Political Elites in Early Republican China: The Parliament of 1913–14." *Journal of Asian Studies* 37 (February 1978): 293–313.

Chesneaux, Jean. *The Chinese Labor Movement*. Translated by H.M. Wright. Stanford, 1968.

Cochran, Sherman. *Big Business in China: Sino-foreign Rivalry in the Cigarette Industry 1890–1930*. Cambridge, 1980.

Ch'ü T'ung-tsu. *Law and Society in Traditional China*. Paris, 1961.

———. *Local Government in China Under the Ch'ing*. Stanford, 1962.

Derrick, Jonathan, *Africa's Slavery Today*. New York, 1975.

Eastman, Lloyd. *The Abortive Revolution: China under Nationalist Rule 1927–37*. Cambridge, 1974.

Eberhard, Wolfram. *Moral and Social Values of the Chinese: Collected Essays*. Taipei, 1971.

———. *Sin and Guilt in Traditional China*. Berkeley, 1967.

———. *Social Mobility in Traditional China*. Leiden, 1966.

Fei Hsiao-t'ung. *Peasant Life in China*. London, 1952.

———. "Relations between City and Village in China." *China Economist* (15 November 1948): 138–39, 149.

Feuerwerker, Albert. *China's Early Industrialization*. New York, 1970.

Fried, Morton. *The Fabric of Chinese Society*. New York, 1953.

Furth, Charlotte, ed. *The Limits of Change: Essays on Conservative Alternatives to Republican China*. Cambridge, 1976.

Garrett, Shirley. "The Chambers of Commerce and the Y.M.C.A." In *The Chinese City Between Two Worlds*. Edited by G(eorge) William Skinner and Mark Elvin. Stanford, 1974, pp. 213–38.

Gernet, Jacques. *Daily Life in China on the Eve of the Mongol Invasion 1250–1276.* Translated by H.M. Wright. Stanford, 1962.

Goode, William J. *World Revolution in Family Patterns.* New York, 1963.

Goodrich, L. Carrington. "Maternal Influence: A Note." *Harvard Journal of Asian Studies* 12 (1948): 226–30.

Handlin, Joanna. "Lu K'un's New Audience." In *Women in Chinese Society.* Edited by Margery Wolf and Roxane Witke. Stanford, 1975, pp. 13–38.

Hsiao Kung-chuan. *Rural China: Imperial Control in the Nineteenth Century.* Seattle, 1967.

Hsueh Chun-te. ed. *Revolutionary Leaders of Modern China.* New York, 1971.

Hucker, Charles. *China's Imperial Past.* Stanford, 1978.

Kopytoff, Igor, and Miers, Suzanne. *Slavery In Africa: Historical and Anthropological Perspectives.* Madison, 1977.

Liang Ch'i-ch'ao. "Chung-kuo nu-li chih-tu." *Ch'ing hua hsüeh pao.* 2 (December 1925): 527–53.

Levy, Howard S. *Chinese Footbinding: The History of a Curious Erotic Custom.* New York, 1966.

Levy, Marion Jr. *The Family Revolution in Modern China.* New York, 1971.

MacKinnon, Steve. "Police Reform in Late Ch'ing Chihli." *Ch'ing-shih wen-ti* 3 (1979): 82-99.

Mallory, Walter. *China: Land of Famine.* New York, 1926.

Mattelart, Armand, and Sigeluart, Seth, eds. *Communication and Class Struggle.* Vol. I *Capitalism and Imperialism.* New York, 1979.

Metzger, Thomas A. *The Internal Organization of the Ch'ing Bureaucracy.* Cambridge, 1973.

Myers, Ramon. *The Chinese Peasant Economy: Agricultural Development in Hopei and Shantung, 1890–1949.* Cambridge, 1970.

Moise, Edward. "Downward Social Mobility in Pre-Revolutionary China." *Modern China* 3 (January 1977): 3–29.

Murphy, Rhoads. "Treaty Ports and Chinese Modernization." In *The Chinese City Between Two Worlds.* Edited by G(eorge) William Skinner and Mark Elvin. Stanford, 1974, pp. 17–72.

Nathan, Andrew. *A History of the China International Famine Relief Commission.* Cambridge, 1965.

———. *Peking Politics, 1918–23.* Berkeley, 1976.

O'Hara, Albert Richard. *The Position of Women in Early China: According to the Lieh Nü Chuan, the Biography of Chinese Women.* Taipei, 1971.

Paul, Diana Y. *Women in Buddhism: Images of the Feminine in the Mahayana Tradition.* Berkeley, 1979.

Perkins, Dwight. *Agricultural Development in China: 1368–1968.* Chicago, 1969.

Rankin, Mary Backus. "The Emergence of Women at the End of the Ch'ing." In *Women in Chinese Society.* Edited by Margery Wolf and Roxane Witke. Stanford, 1975, pp. 39–66.

———."Leading Families in Two Chekiang Marketing Towns." *Ch'ing-shih wen-t'i* 3 (November 1977): 67–104.

Rawski, Evelyn S. *Education and Popular Literacy in Ch'ing China.* Ann Arbor, 1979.

Schran, Peter. "China's Demographic Evolution 1850–1953 Reconsidered." *China Quarterly,* no. 75 (September 1978), pp. 639–46.

Sheridan, James. *China in Disintegration.* New York, 1975.

———. *Chinese Warlord: The Career of Feng Yü-hsiang.* Stanford, 1966.

Shin, Linda, "Women and Reform." In *Reform in Nineteenth Century China.* Edited by Paul Cohen and John Schrecker. Cambridge, 1976, pp. 245–57.

Spence, Jonathan D. *The Death of Woman Wang*. New York, 1978.

Strand, David. "Streetcar Conductors, Rickshaw Pullers, and Policemen: Peking in the 1920's." Lecture at Columbia University, April 24, 1979.

Sun, E-tu Zen, and de Francis, John, eds. *Chinese Social History: Translations of Selected Studies*. New York, 1966.

Tadeo Sakai. "Confucianism and Popular Educational Works." In *Self and Society in Ming Thought*. Edited by W(illiam) Theodore de Bary. New York, 1970, pp. 331–66.

Tang Tsou and Ho P'ing-ti, eds. *China in Crisis: China's Heritage and the Communist Political System*. 2 Volumes. Chicago, 1968.

Teitelbaum, Michael. 'The Relevance of Demographic Transition Theory for Developing Countries." *Science* 188 (April-June 1975): 420–25.

Tien Tsung. "Women Who Do Not Marry," *Orient* 2 (July 1952): 41–43.

Topley, Marjorie. "Marriage Resistance in Rural Kwangtung." In *Studies in Chinese Society*. Edited by Arthur Wolf. Stanford, 1978, pp. 247–68.

Tsu Yu-yue. *The Spirit of Chinese Philanthropy*. New York: Columbia University Studies in History, Economics, and Public Law, 1912.

Van der Sprenkel, Sybille. *Legal Institutions in Manchu China: A Sociological Analysis*. London, 1971.

Wakeman, Frederic Jr. *The Fall of Imperial China*. New York, 1975.

Wang Chi-min and Wu Lien-teh. *History of Chinese Medicine*. Shanghai, 1936.

Watson, James L. "Chattel Slavery in Chinese Peasant Society: A Comparative Approach." *Ethnology* 15 (October 1976): 361–75.

Werner, Edward Theodore Chalmers. *A History of Chinese Civilization*. Shanghai, 1940.

Wilbur, C(larence) Martin. *Slavery in China During the Former Han Dynasty*. Chicago, 1943.

Wilkinson, H(iram) P(arkes). *The Family in Classical China*. Shanghai, 1926.

Winckler, Sophia Sa. "Family and Community in Urban Taiwan: Social Status and Demographic Strategy among Taipei Households 1885–1935." Ph.D. Dissertation, Harvard University, 1975.

Witke, Roxane. "Mao Tse-t'ung, Women and Suicide." In *Women in Chinese Society*. Edited by Margery Wolf and Roxane Witke. Stanford, 1975, pp. 89–110.

Wolf, Arthur. "The Women of Hai-shan: A Demographic Portrait." In *Women in Chinese Society*. Edited by Margery Wolf and Roxane Witke. Stanford, 1975, pp. 89–110.

Wolf, Margery. "Chinese Women: Old Skills in New Contexts." In *Women, Culture, and Society*. Edited by Michelle Zimbalist Rosaldo and Louise Lamphere. Stanford, 1974, pp. 157–72.

———. *House of Lim: A Study of a Chinese Farm Family*. Englewood Cliffs, N.J., 1968.

———. "Women and Suicide in China." In *Women in Chinese Society*. Edited by Margery Wolf and Roxane Witke. Stanford, 1975, pp. 111–42.

———. Women and the Family in Rural Taiwan. Stanford, 1972.

Wright, Mary C. *China in Revolution: The First Phase 1900–1913*. New Haven, 1968.

Yang, Martin C. *Chinese Social Structure*. Taipei, 1969.

Sexology and Prostitution

Bullough, Vern. *The History of Prostitution*. New York, 1964.

Chou, Eric. *The Dragon and the Phoenix*. New York, 1970.

Henriques, Fernando. *Prostitution and Society: A Survey*. London, 1962.

Rubin, Gayle. "The Traffic in Women: Notes on the Political Economy of Sex." In *Towards a New Anthropology of Women.* Edited by Rayna Reiter. New York, 1975, pp. 157–210.

Schlegel, Gustaaf. *Histoire de la prostitution en Chine.* Rouen, 1880.

Van Gulik, Robert H. *Sexual Life in Ancient China: A Preliminary Survey of Chinese Sex and Society from 1500 B.C. to 1644 A.D.* Leiden, 1974.

Woo, Chan-cheng. *L'érotologie de la Chine: tradition Chinoise de l'érotisme.* Translated by F. Albertini. Paris, 1963.

Literary Criticism

Hsia Chih-tsing. *The Classic Chinese Novel.* New York, 1968.

———. *Modern Chinese Fiction.* New Haven, 1974.

Hsia Tsi-an. *The Gate of Darkness: Studies on the Leftist Literary Movement in China.* Seattle, 1968.

Lee, Leo Ou-fan. *The Romantic Generation of Chinese Writers.* Cambridge, 1975.

Link, E(dward) Perry. "The Rise of Modern Popular Fiction in Shanghai." Ph.D. Dissertation, Harvard University, 1976.

Liu Wu-chi. *An Introduction to Chinese Literature.* Bloomington, Indiana, 1966.

Lu Hsün. *A Brief History of Chinese Fiction.* Translated by Gladys Yang. Peking, 1976.

Schyn, Joseph. *1500 Modern Chinese Novels and Plays.* Peiping, 1948.

INDEX

Abandonment, child, 46
Abortion, 18–19,54,75–76
Adoption: attitude toward, 39–40;
    brothel, 9,19; disguised slavery,
    34,48,71–73; forms, 38–40; fu-
    ture daughter-in-law (*yang hsi*),
    39; motives, 39,40,55; *mui tsai,*
    39; real daughter (*yang nü*),
    39,55; reform, 34,86–87
Andrews, Elizabeth, 34
Art of the Bedchamber, 15
Ayscough, Florence, 20–22

Begging, 8,55. See also Work,
    women's
*Biographies of Famous Women (Lieh
    nü chuan),* 29,47
Biographies of local histories, 29–30
"Blame" novels, as source, 2
Boxer Rebellion, 67,78,82
British Abolition Society's Hong Kong
    Anti-Mui Tsai Branch, 81
Brothels: change in the twentieth cen-
    tury, 65–68; control in, 17; dis-
    tricts, 67; history, 4–5; levels, 5–
    8,67–69; licensing and registra-
    tion, 5–6,65; names, 9–10; orga-
    nization and personnel, 8–10,10–
    12; prices and population, 10–11;
    routine, 8–9. See also Prostitution
Buddhism, 35
Bullies, local, 82–83
Businessmen, new, 58

Cash (*wen*), equivalents, 91 n.22
Caste. See Mean; Social Class
Chambers of Commerce, 58,63
Chang T'ien-yi, "A Summer Night's
    Dream," 75,82
Chefoo, 85

Chiang K'ai-shek, 62
Childhood, 37–41. See also Infanticide
China: changes 1911–36, 51; condi-
    tions in North China, 53–54
Chinese Anti-Kidnapping Society of
    Shanghai, 81
Classics for Girls (Nü erh ching), 29
Communists, 52,57,89
Concubinage, 16,23,33,49,81,86
Confucianism, 26,29,52,82,84–85
Contraception, 18–19,54,75. See also
    Pregnancy
Courtesan: description, 5,8–11; trans-
    formation, 36,65,77
Cultural imperialism, 60–61
Custom. See *Li*

Daughter of Han, 11,19,35,38,42,44
"Debt" prostitutes, 70. See also
    Pawning
Divorce, 42. See also Marriage
Door of Hope (*Chi liang so*), 83
Dostoevsky, 59
*Dream of the Red Chamber (Hung lou
    meng),* 18,23,24,38,43,45
Dress: traditional, 5,6,17; twentieth
    century, 59,60,61

Education: end examination system,
    60,78; literacy of prostitutes, 15;
    of women, 79; western learning,
    60
Entertainment: and art associated with
    prostitutes, 4–6,8,23,51,64,65
Erotic and pornographic literature,
    1,15,22–23

"Face," 22. See also *Li*
Famine, 45–47,72–73
Fei Hsiao-t'ung, 62